APA Style Simplified

As always, for Linda, Agatha, and Simon,
who give style to my life.

APA Style Simplified

Writing in Psychology, Education, Nursing, and Sociology

Bernard C. Beins

A John Wiley & Sons, Ltd., Publication

This edition first published 2012
© 2012 John Wiley & Sons, Inc

Wiley-Blackwell is an imprint of John Wiley & Sons, formed by the merger of Wiley's global
Scientific, Technical and Medical business with Blackwell Publishing.

Registered Office
John Wiley & Sons Ltd, The Atrium, Southern Gate, Chichester, West Sussex, PO19 8SQ, UK

Editorial Offices
350 Main Street, Malden, MA 02148-5020, USA
9600 Garsington Road, Oxford, OX4 2DQ, UK
The Atrium, Southern Gate, Chichester, West Sussex, PO19 8SQ, UK

For details of our global editorial offices, for customer services, and for information about
how to apply for permission to reuse the copyright material in this book please see our website
at www.wiley.com/wiley-blackwell.

The right of Bernard C. Beins to be identified as the author of this work has been asserted
in accordance with the UK Copyright, Designs and Patents Act 1988.

Wiley also publishes its books in a variety of electronic formats. Some content that appears
in print may not be available in electronic books.

Designations used by companies to distinguish their products are often claimed as trademarks.
All brand names and product names used in this book are trade names, service marks,
trademarks or registered trademarks of their respective owners. The publisher is not associated
with any product or vendor mentioned in this book. This publication is designed to provide
accurate and authoritative information in regard to the subject matter covered. It is sold on the
understanding that the publisher is not engaged in rendering professional services. If professional
advice or other expert assistance is required, the services of a competent professional should
be sought.

Library of Congress Cataloging-in-Publication Data applied for

Hardback ISBN: 9780470672327
Paperback ISBN: 9780470671238

A catalogue record for this book is available from the British Library.

Set in 10.5/13pt Minion by SPi Publisher Services, Pondicherry, India
Printed in Singapore by Ho Printing Singapore Pte Ltd

1   2012

Contents

Preface

When you learn to write in APA style, it can seem as if you are learning to write in a foreign language. The endless details that you need to know can be overwhelming. In reality, though, learning to produce a paper in APA style does not need to be all that difficult. There certainly are details that you have to pay attention to, but APA style is designed so that readers know what will appear in your paper and where they can find it. If you keep that in mind, the process becomes easier.

I remember writing my first APA-style paper as an undergraduate. I was as mystified by it as everybody else was. In fact, I remember thinking that nobody really wrote like that. So I basically ignored APA style and wrote what I thought was appropriate. The professor didn't share my perspective and the paper that was returned to me was colored in red marks throughout. So I wised up and decided that maybe people do use this style after all. And it is true: Professionals in many fields use APA style in their communications.

By the time you finish using this book, you will be proficient in APA style. This book is unlike some other guides to APA style in that it does more than simply present a set of rules to follow. My belief is that you can follow rules more easily and effectively if you understand the purpose for the rules. So each chapter in the book tells you not only how to present your ideas but also why it makes sense to do so. In the end, your manuscript will have appropriate formatting, which is important, but it will also be well constructed, meaningful, and (I hope) interesting to the reader.

It would be unrealistic to think that you will know every detail of APA style after using this book. The *Publication Manual of the American Psychological Association* (6th ed.), as it is formally known, consists of 290 pages, including the front matter and the index. It is possible to pack a lot of detail into 290 pages, and the American Psychological Association has done so. But the number of details that you actually need to know is not all that great. It seems so at the beginning, but in reality there is a fairly small number that relates to papers you are likely to write.

I tell my Research Team students that if anyone ever hands in a complete APA-style paper without a single deviation from APA style, they will earn an automatic *A* in the course. Naturally, nobody has even come close. I know that there are so many nitpicking details that nobody is likely to know them all. In fact, I tell my students that I hope nobody gets the automatic *A* because there are more important things to do with their lives than memorizing the *Publication Manual*. Still, they do a very creditable job writing their papers that are generally consistent with APA style in virtually all respects and are coherent and interesting as well.

How to Use This Book

This book is largely a reference guide that will help you to format and structure papers. At the same time, it presents useful guidance about the characteristics of high-quality writing that is both competent regarding the use of the English language and consistent with APA style. Your final product will be stronger if you attend to the material on creating compelling prose and to the technical material relating to APA style.

If you are writing a term paper that presents information on what others have studied and reported but that does not involve your own original research, you are likely to benefit from the material in chapters 1 and 2, which relate to high-quality scientific writing; chapters 3 and 7, which relate to introducing the topic you are addressing and integrating that information in a coherent package; and chapter 8, which involves the formatting of reference citations. Some parts of chapter 9, dealing with formatting, will also be helpful.

If you are working on a research project, you will benefit from the material in the chapters already mentioned. In addition, there is relevant information in chapters 4, 5, and 6, which deal with the details of your research and your results.

After you have completed your project, if you are creating a poster presentation, chapter 10 will be helpful. If you are preparing to give an oral presentation, chapter 11 will give you guidance. If you are interested in Internet or electronic publication, chapter 12 will be useful.

Finally, there are two appendixes with a sample research paper in each. In Appendix A, you will see a research paper with common APA-style errors.

You may want to glance through this appendix to see if you have fallen prey to these errors, which I have found to be the most common among my own students. Appendix B is a corrected version of the material in Appendix A.

By paying attention to the guidance that this book provides, you will be able to produce written papers and posters and will know how to organize and deliver oral presentations. You should also gain a sense of what you want to communicate and how you want to convey it in a way that other researchers will recognize as competent and professional.

Acknowledgments

Writing sometimes seems like solitary work, but that task is ultimately followed by a flurry of activity on the part of many people. The book you are reading may have started with a single keystroke I made on a computer keyboard, but it would not have appeared as you see it without a coordination of effort. I am grateful for the help I received throughout the production process. The people who contributed in significant (but hidden) ways include the hard-working editorial staff at Wiley-Blackwell, including my editor, Matt Bennett; the project editor, Julia Kirk; and the senior editorial assistant, Nicole Benevenia, and my copy editor with an eagle eye, Joanna Pyke.

I also thank the reviewers who read preliminary drafts and made helpful comments to improve the book. Although it feels good when reviewers give high praise to the work I've produced, the critical comments that they provide invariably lead to a more useful and higher-quality book. As such, I give my thanks to the anonymous reviewers who helped clarify my ideas and my prose.

Finally, I must admit that my wife, Linda, is really the brains of the operation. She is a marvelous contributor to all of my projects. This project would not have unfolded without her as wonderfully as it did.

1

Writing Professionally

Write what matters. If you don't care about what you're writing, neither will your readers.

Judy Reeves

I'm not a very good writer, but I'm an excellent rewriter.

James Michener

When people write professionally in the social, educational, or health sciences, they are telling a story about people. But scientists are people, too, complete with individual personalities, likes and dislikes, and ordinary human qualities. Their personalities affect what they do and how they do it. As such, "science writing is not so much about science, but about people—human problems and their solutions, curiosity and discovery" (Holland, 2007). In this book, you will learn how to convey your thoughts on the important problems and solutions relating to people.

It would be hard to overstate how important it is to write effectively. Writing constitutes one of the "3 Rs" of a basic education: reading, writing and 'rithmetic. In the world of business, success is dependent, in part, on effective writing. For high-level positions, "writing is a 'threshold skill' for both employment and promotion" (College Board, 2004, p. 3). In one survey, many companies noted that writing was important in hiring. One respondent asserted that, "in most cases, writing ability could be your ticket in … or it could be your ticket out" (College Board, 2004, p. 3). Potential

APA Style Simplified: Writing in Psychology, Education, Nursing, and Sociology,
First Edition. Bernard C. Beins.
© 2012 John Wiley & Sons, Inc. Published 2012 by John Wiley & Sons, Inc.

employees who do not write well are unlikely to be hired and, if they are hired, they are unlikely to be promoted.

Graduate school admission may also depend on writing effectiveness. Graduate programs routinely request essays as part of the application process. This writing is "often used to make final selections of students with similar GPAs and standardized test scores. If you are on the borderline of being accepted and the admissions committee could go either way, a sterling essay can increase your chances of success considerably" (American Psychological Association, 2007, p. 132).

More immediately, the type of writing presented in this book focuses on the technical style presented in the *Publication Manual of the American Psychological Association* (American Psychological Association, 2010). In the end, you will develop skill in writing in APA style, presenting your ideas with clarity and logic in a manner that will engage the reader.

Most of us find people interesting and are eager to learn why they behave the way they do. But readers do not want to fight through dull and meaningless writing. As writers, our biggest hurdle involves turning complex, technical concepts into prose that others can appreciate.

Writing successfully is not easy. It requires knowledge of the topic we are addressing; judicious selection of the best words, phrases, and sentences; and editing and revising what we have composed. If there were a magical formula that we could use to generate good prose, everybody would succeed in communicating even complex and hard-to-understand ideas. If you have read the work of scientists, though, you will have discovered that, much of the time, scientific writing is dense and impenetrable. Many writers hide interesting concepts inside packages of dull prose.

Furthermore, when you write a paper, not only do you have to make your points clearly, but you have to do it in APA style. This book will focus on writing effectively within the technical constraints of APA style.

How Does Professional Writing Differ From Other Kinds of Writing?

If you are trying to write like a professional, your style will be unlike much of the writing that you have done in the past. When we write professionally, we usually attempt to convey specific information with a great deal of precision, minimizing ambiguity and the possibility of being misunderstood. The adage to say what you mean and mean what you say is highly appropriate for technical writing. You want your reader to understand the points you believe are important, and you want the reader to know exactly what you intend to say.

In other forms of writing, the emphasis may be on crafting artistic prose. The writer attempts to impress the reader with both content and style. The words that Shakespeare wrote for Macbeth illustrate the point. Macbeth lamented that life "is a tale told by an idiot, full of sound and fury, signifying nothing." These poetic words convey Macbeth's despair. However, Shakespeare's style would not be appropriate for a scientist because the style of science is to be straightforward and unambiguous so the reader does not have to puzzle through the words to find meaning in them.

Psychologists often receive training in how to write objective, scientific papers. Unfortunately, the writing style is often "bloodless" (Josselson & Lieblich, 1996, p. 651), meaning that it is not particularly engaging. Sommer (2006) has encouraged psychologists to learn to write with color and style for lay audiences without sacrificing accuracy. He also implied that the writing style in academic journals need not be dreary.

In scientific writing, we focus on the content of the message. The point is not to impress the reader with the prose, but to render the prose invisible while making the content foremost. This type of writing can be as difficult to do well as literary writing because you need to be concise without omitting important information; you need to choose your words carefully so they engage the reader without obscuring your point; you need to say enough to let your reader understand your message without being repetitive.

Another difference among the various types of writing is that, when we write scientifically or technically, we generally rely on a vocabulary specific to the topic at hand. Professionals understand this wording, but others are not likely to be as conversant with the terminology. This is one of the reasons that scientific writing has the reputation of being incomprehensible—you need to know the jargon. (The concepts are also complex and may be hard to understand, which does not help.) Actually, technical terms are helpful because they let us communicate complex ideas clearly in a few words, although if you do not know the meanings of the words, the prose is meaningless or, at best, difficult.

Using APA Style

A further difference between scientific or technical writing and less formal writing is that, in science, authors typically follow a specific format in preparing reports. In this book, we will follow the guidelines that appear in the

Table 1.1   Typical Sections in an APA-Style Research Report

Section of the report	What the section contains
Title page	The title of the paper, the names of authors, and the affiliations of the authors
Abstract	A brief overview of the entire project of about 150 to 250 words
Introduction	The background and logic of the study, including previous research that led to this project
Method	Minute details of how the study proceeded, including descriptions of participants, apparatus, and materials, and what researchers and participants actually did during the study
Results	A detailed statement of the statistics and other results of the study
Discussion	What the results tell us about thought and behavior
References	Where to find the work cited in the paper that relates to the present study

Publication Manual of the American Psychological Association (American Psychological Association, 2010), commonly just called APA style. To begin with, in APA style, research reports usually include seven sections, as described in Table 1.1.

The path that you will take in writing a paper for a class parallels that of submitting a manuscript to a journal. Most of the time, if a writer submits to a journal editor a manuscript that deviates greatly from APA style, the editor may reject the manuscript immediately as unsuitable for publication. In some cases, editors work with authors so that the final version of the manuscript is consistent with APA style (Brewer, Scherzer, Van Raalte, Petitpas, & Andersen, 2001). Similarly, in a class, instructors often insist on APA style and often work with students trying to learn the intricacies of this kind of writing.

In addition, editors have commented that deviations from APA style often accompany problems with the content of a manuscript. So if you create a manuscript that fails to follow APA style, an instructor who is familiar with (and used to) APA style may assume that you paid as little attention to your ideas as you did to the way you expressed them. In the workplace, employers have expressed similar sentiments, that poor writing reflects poor thought (College Board, 2004).

According to the research of Brewer et al. (2001) on the use and the importance of APA style, writers are likely to deviate from APA style in their presentation of research results and in citing references. So you should pay particular attention to these facets of your writing. If you write a paper in APA style that does not involve empirical research and data analysis, APA style can still apply. The structure of your paper is likely to have elements in common with the Introduction, Discussion, and References sections of a research paper, which appear in later chapters. Once you learn the basics of APA style, writing an effective paper might be easier than you anticipated because you will have a good sense of what belongs in a paper and where it goes.

As you write professionally, keep in mind that readers are willing to be convinced with persuasive arguments, but you have to convince them. Scientific writing entails presenting a series of logical arguments that follow from one another. At the end, your good logic is going to make a believer out of your reader. If we are going to accept the process of science, it means that when a writer offers a logical argument that is supported by good data, we should be willing to accept that argument.

Making a Credible Argument

The difference between scientific writing and other writing has to do with the nature of how psychologists attempt to persuade readers. In everyday life, if you want to change somebody's mind about something, there are several ways of doing it. One is to appeal to authority. That is, by quoting an expert (i.e., an authority), you can often convince people to believe you. After all, experts know more than others in their field of expertise. Unfortunately, experts can be wrong.

You can also appeal to what "everybody" knows is true; some things are so obvious, they must be true. Unfortunately (again), some things that people "know" to be true simply aren't true.

You can also appeal to others' emotions. Politicians and advertisers do this all the time. Unfortunately (again), conclusions based on emotional appeals can make a person feel good about a decision that, ultimately, proves to be troublesome. Furthermore, such conclusions are often not very stable (Petty & Cacioppo, 1986).

We should not simply believe the experts (even though they are probably right more than they are wrong in their areas of expertise); they should have to convince us with logical arguments. We should not simply trust our senses (even though a lot of what we feel to be true has some validity). We should not simply believe in what makes us feel good or reject what makes us feel bad; it should have logical validity.

When trying to convince your reader of your arguments, you should engage the reader in critical evaluation of your ideas. Research has revealed that persuasion based on logic and on attention to important details leads to greater and longer-term acceptance of an argument. This is the type of persuasion that you should strive for in your writing.

Different Types of Communication

If you want to communicate with your audience, you need to know what your audience expects. Depending on whether you are writing, speaking, or presenting visually, your approach will differ somewhat, even if the underlying message is the same.

Written Communication

If you are writing a formal, APA-style research report, as you would for publication in a journal, your reader will expect a structured presentation with considerable detail. The advantage of such a written presentation is that your reader can go back and review the background you cite, review your methodology to make sure it is sound, evaluate your results to judge if they are appropriate, and see if your conclusions are justified from your results and if they relate to the ideas you presented in your Introduction. A written document is a permanent exposition that the reader can go back to at will.

Professionals (including professors) expect the writing to be free from colloquial or informal expressions and to be entirely grammatical. You should choose your words carefully because they are lasting expressions of your ideas.

Oral Communication

In contrast, if you are delivering that same research in an oral presentation, you cannot possibly pack the same level of detail and expect your audience to understand your ideas. Working memory is limited to a small amount of information. So if you are talking to people in an audience, it does not make sense to introduce as many ideas as you would in writing; your audience cannot go back to review what you have already said. They are forced to listen to your ideas in the present and can keep track of only a few ideas.

In an oral presentation, you should limit yourself to three or four main points you want your listeners to remember. You can introduce minor points to help reinforce the major ideas, but your audience will have a hard time keeping the details in memory. Professional speakers suggest that you tell your audience what you are going to say, then say it, and finally tell them what you just told them. There is something to this philosophy, although in a research presentation, you should not be quite so simplistic. You should establish the framework of your presentation and repeat critical points when appropriate. Still, in the short period of time allotted to oral presentations, usually 10 to 15 min, you are limited in the amount of information you can convey, just as the audience is limited in its ability to comprehend your ideas.

Poster Presentations

Yet another medium of expression is visual. Increasingly, research conferences are relying on poster presentations for reporting research findings. In this form of communication, you present all your information in a small display that might be about 4 ft × 6 ft (i.e., 1.3 m × 2 m) in size. The dimensions vary from one conference to another, but the amount of space always seems to be smaller than you would want.

One of the worst things you can do is to fill the poster with text. Nobody wants to fight through a poster with endless strings of sentences. The viewer is typically interested in your main points. Fortunately, during such a presentation, the author of the poster is usually present, so if viewers want to know more details than are available on the poster, they can simply ask. The use of tables, figures, bulleted points, and other eye-catching features is a good idea in a poster. However, you should avoid attractive, but irrelevant, visual features.

So, for a poster, you should present the main points with as little text as you can get away with. Visual elements are often a more meaningful way to make your points accessible. The result is often more information than in an oral presentation, but less than in a complete APA-style research report. It helps when the researcher is present to clear up any misconceptions that arise because not all the information is available on the poster. Furthermore, if you are presenting a poster, you can create a handout that resembles an

APA-style manuscript. In this way, interested people can get the gist of your research and can ask you any questions that come to mind right away. Then they can take your written handout and attend later to the level of detail they desire.

Internet Publishing

A relatively new option for communicating your ideas is through the Internet. Web presentations combine various features of traditional manuscripts and of visual displays, but there are some additional elements that foster effective communication. A web-based presentation allows easy use of visual elements that are often too costly to include in printed manuscripts. In addition, you can use hyperlinks with your text to refer the reader to related web material or to references.

A simple web page is fairly easy to create if all you need is to present text, figures, or pictures, and hyperlinked text. It is helpful to know the code for the language of the web, HTML (HyperText Markup Language), but with the authoring software on the market, knowing HTML is not absolutely necessary. Fortunately, it is fairly easy to learn. You can even save word-processed documents in HTML format, although generating a well-formatted web page from a word processor can be tricky.

Effective Communication

A professor named Denis Dutton held a bad-writing contest for a few years. The sentence that motivated him to begin the contest appears below; it was about an attempt at educational reform. The prose, which was not intended to be bad, was absolutely incomprehensible. (You should not feel embarrassed if you don't understand it. I don't understand it, either.)

> [It] would delegitimate the decisive, if spontaneous, disclosure of the complicity of liberal American institutions of higher learning with the state's brutal conduct of the war in Vietnam and the consequent call for opening the university to meet the demands by hitherto marginalized constituencies of American society for enfranchisement. (Dutton, 1999)

One of the goals of this book is an attempt to prevent you from writing such incomprehensible prose.

No matter what you choose as your medium of presentation, there are some characteristics of good communication to remember. First, you should establish your theme and organize your thoughts around it, which requires that you know what you want to say. It is tempting sometimes to start writing without a coherent idea of your message. If you operate this way, your writing may meander toward irrelevant topics.

Second, if you want to communicate effectively, you should make sure that your grammar is flawless and that your selection of words is judicious. When your writing is technically competent, your reader will not be distracted from your message by having to figure out what you mean. You also need to go back to your work to edit and revise it. It helps to reread your work when it is not fresh in your own mind; sometimes you can spot problems that were not initially apparent. In addition, your writing may benefit if you ask somebody to read your work and explain to you what is unclear. Mark Twain recognized the importance of revising your work: "The time to begin writing an article is when you have finished it to your satisfaction. By that time you begin to clearly and logically perceive what it is you really want to say."

Finally, it is important to remember that even lengthy manuscripts begin with a single sentence. In order to maximize the effectiveness of your writing, you should set up a schedule and a process. B. F. Skinner is a good example; he was an early bird, so he arose and did his writing for a few hours in the morning, a practice that he continued right up until his death.

Establishing Good Writing Habits

Find a place where you can concentrate free of distraction, at a time when you are clear-headed. If you are a night owl, that may be the best time for you to write; if you are an early-morning lark, that would be a good time. In either case, you should establish a routine. Writing does not happen until you do it. And when you develop your routine, remember to positively reinforce yourself. Identify a goal for your writing session and reward yourself when you reach it. So you might decide to explore and write about a given topic for 30 min. After 30 min, you should reward yourself with a break.

You may need to shape your behavior first, though, so you might need to start with a shorter work period, gradually extending it until you identify the longest period of time during which you can write effectively. Psychologists have identified a phenomenon called *post-reinforcement pause*. It refers to a period of time after a reinforcement when the animal (including the human animal) stops working toward another reinforcement (Felton & Lyon, 1966). You should make sure that your post-reinforcement pauses are not too lengthy.

By developing good writing habits, you will have taken the first step toward successful communicating. The task is often not easy, but the results are eminently satisfying.

In the next chapters, we will explore how you can develop your ideas, connect them to what others have already written, and express them in a style that reflects a sophisticated knowledge of psychology, all in APA style. In the end, you will have an impact on your audience when you write and when you speak about psychology.

Ethical Writing

Academic integrity is a concept that guides ethical writing and more broadly addresses cheating, plagiarism, and even denying others access to scholarly resources. In this section you will encounter examples and tips to help you avoid plagiarism, but it would be a good idea to read your university's policy on academic integrity. This section begins with an excerpt from a scholarly source and a paragraph that attempts to paraphrase that source (this example is inspired by the University of Kent's psychology department web page at http://www.kent.ac.uk/psychology/learning-resources/plagiarism.html).

In Figure 1.1 you can see an outline of the mistakes in the paraphrased version and then a way to rewrite it, which is described in Figure 1.2.

Scholarly Excerpt

According to self-determination theory (Deci & Ryan, 1985, 1991) individuals who perform an activity out of choice and pleasure regulate their behavior in a self-determined manner. In contrast, individuals who participate in different activities out of internal and/or external pressures regulate their behavior in a non-self-determined fashion. Throughout the past two decades, much research has shown that self-determined motivation is a useful concept to understand human behavior. (Senecal, Vallerand, & Guay, 2001, p. 178)

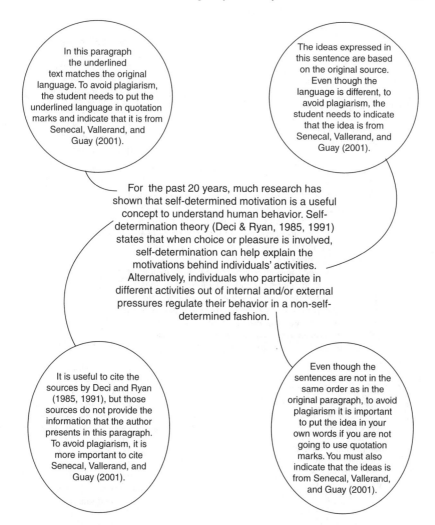

In this paragraph the underlined text matches the original language. To avoid plagiarism, the student needs to put the underlined language in quotation marks and indicate that it is from Senecal, Vallerand, and Guay (2001).

The ideas expressed in this sentence are based on the original source. Even though the language is different, to avoid plagiarism, the student needs to indicate that the idea is from Senecal, Vallerand, and Guay (2001).

For the past 20 years, much research has shown that self-determined motivation is a useful concept to understand human behavior. Self-determination theory (Deci & Ryan, 1985, 1991) states that when choice or pleasure is involved, self-determination can help explain the motivations behind individuals' activities. Alternatively, individuals who participate in different activities out of internal and/or external pressures regulate their behavior in a non-self-determined fashion.

It is useful to cite the sources by Deci and Ryan (1985, 1991), but those sources do not provide the information that the author presents in this paragraph. To avoid plagiarism, it is more important to cite Senecal, Vallerand, and Guay (2001).

Even though the sentences are not in the same order as in the original paragraph, to avoid plagiarism it is important to put the idea in your own words if you are not going to use quotation marks. You must also indicate that the ideas is from Senecal, Vallerand, and Guay (2001).

Figure 1.1   Avoiding plagiarism.

Attempted Paraphrase

For the last 20 years, much research has shown that self-determined motivation is a useful concept to understand human behavior. Self-determination theory (Deci & Ryan, 1985, 1991) states that, when choice or pleasure is involved, self-determination can help explain the motivations behind individuals' activities. Alternatively, individuals who participate in different activities out of internal and/or external pressures regulate their behavior in a non-self-determined fashion.

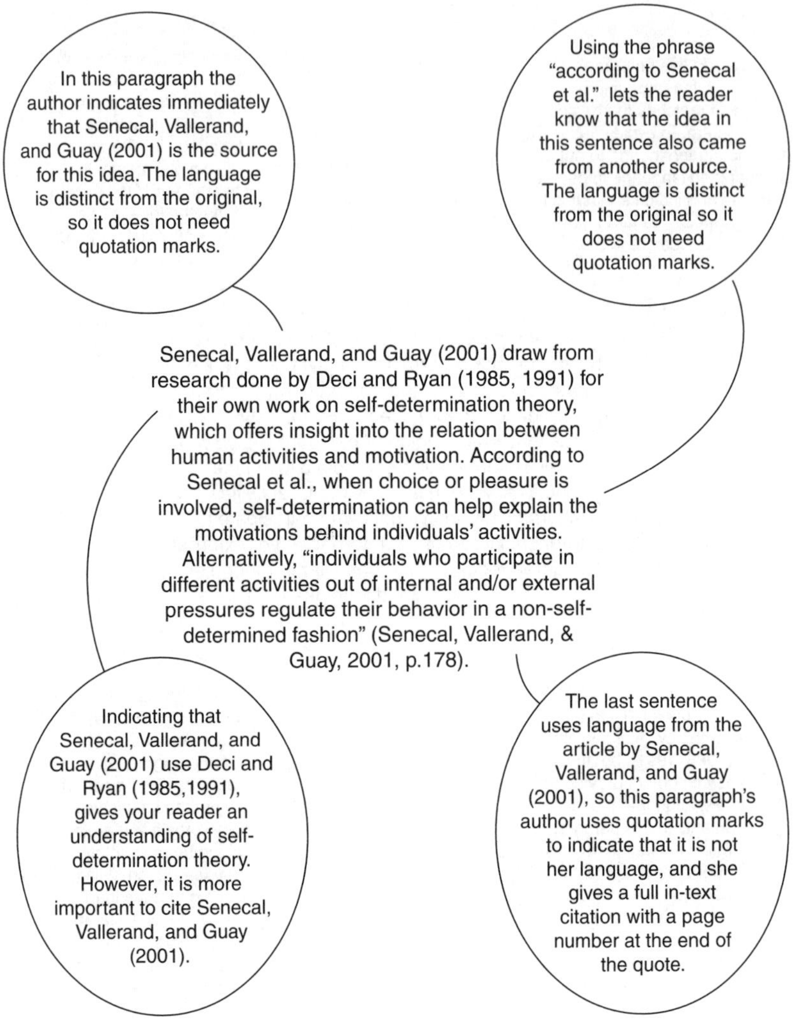

In this paragraph the author indicates immediately that Senecal, Vallerand, and Guay (2001) is the source for this idea. The language is distinct from the original, so it does not need quotation marks.

Using the phrase "according to Senecal et al." lets the reader know that the idea in this sentence also came from another source. The language is distinct from the original so it does not need quotation marks.

Senecal, Vallerand, and Guay (2001) draw from research done by Deci and Ryan (1985, 1991) for their own work on self-determination theory, which offers insight into the relation between human activities and motivation. According to Senecal et al., when choice or pleasure is involved, self-determination can help explain the motivations behind individuals' activities. Alternatively, "individuals who participate in different activities out of internal and/or external pressures regulate their behavior in a non-self-determined fashion" (Senecal, Vallerand, & Guay, 2001, p.178).

Indicating that Senecal, Vallerand, and Guay (2001) use Deci and Ryan (1985,1991), gives your reader an understanding of self-determination theory. However, it is more important to cite Senecal, Vallerand, and Guay (2001).

The last sentence uses language from the article by Senecal, Vallerand, and Guay (2001), so this paragraph's author uses quotation marks to indicate that it is not her language, and she gives a full in-text citation with a page number at the end of the quote.

Figure 1.2 How plagiarism has been avoided.

Paraphrase Rewrite

Senecal, Vallerand, & Guay (2001) draw from research done by Deci & Ryan (1985, 1991) for their own work on self-determination theory, which offers insight into the relationship between human activities and motivation. According to Senecal et al., when choice or pleasure is involved, self-determination can help explain the motivations behind individuals' activities. Alternatively, "individuals who participate in different activities out of internal and/or external pressures regulate their behavior in a non-self-determined fashion" (Senecal, Vallerand, & Guay, 2001, p. 178).

Whether intentional or unintentional, plagiarism is a very serious infraction. *Plagiarism* is the use or representation of someone else's idea or language as your own. This can include

- summarizing someone else's idea without giving that person credit;
- using someone else's language without giving that person credit;
- using someone else's language without quotation marks, even if you give that person credit for the idea;
- taking work that someone else wrote for you and presenting it as your own.

However, scholars do not consider it plagiarism if you present information that is *common knowledge* without a citation. That is, if you offer information that you expect an average person would know, such as the temperature at which water freezes or who the fifth United States president was, then you can include that information without needing to cite any sources.

Unfortunately, the margins of common knowledge are not always clear. For example, what is considered common knowledge might be different for psychologists, sociologists, educators, and health professionals. If there is any doubt, you are always safe in citing your sources.

You should become familiar with what is and isn't plagiarism not only because you may face severe consequences for plagiarizing but also because including citations and references in your academic scholarship can strengthen your work: It reflects your awareness of scholarly research that points to the same conclusion.

Referencing perspectives that contradict your stance can benefit your work, too. Showing your audience that you are aware of, and have evaluated, research that presents arguments or conclusions that differ from yours indicates that you have explored multiple perspectives and still consider yours to be the strongest.

So you might forget to cite a source when you are writing your paper, or you might have taken notes but forgotten to write down the source of those notes. Regardless of your intentions, the first example is plagiarism and the second could become plagiarism. Consequently, preventing plagiarism starts when you are in the preliminary research phase and continues through the research and writing process.

Each time you take notes, you want to be able to connect those notes to a specific source. There are different systems you can use to do this, and through your own research and writing you can develop a system that works best for you. For some people, recording a source's complete citation information and then writing notes keeps everything in one place and makes it less likely that either the citation or the notes will be lost or separated. Almost all library catalogs and search engines allow you to email or print citations, and through some article databases you can email or print out entire articles. However, should you email or print citations, you then need to figure out how to connect the citations with your notes about that source.

In any case, you must recognize the importance of keeping track of your sources at the initial research phases and throughout your writing project. Not only can this strategy prevent plagiarism—intentional or unintentional—it can also be more efficient in the long run. There are few things as frustrating as knowing you've summarized, paraphrased, or quoted a source but not knowing which source it is, which causes you to spend time reading through articles or even revisiting the library to retrieve a source you had already returned.

Finally, it is possible to plagiarize from oneself. This phenomenon is called self-plagiarism, and it is not acceptable. Essentially, it is not considered appropriate to lift material from one paper you have written and insert it into a new paper as if it were new. This caution may be more relevant when authors publish their papers in journals, but your professors may have similar policies against your handing in a paper that contains work that you had written previously.

The ethical guidelines set forth by the APA note that in discussions of theory and methodology, some repetition of your earlier work may be appropriate, but the APA cautions minimizing the overlap with your earlier writing and letting readers know when you have taken material from something you wrote before.

2

Elements of Style

Agatha M. Beins

Social criticism begins with grammar and the re-establishing of meanings.

Octavio Paz

Easy reading is damned hard writing.

Nathaniel Hawthorne

A panda walks into a café. He orders a sandwich, eats it, then draws a gun and proceeds to shoot through the ceiling.

"Why?" asks the confused waiter, as the panda makes toward the exit. The panda produces a badly punctuated wildlife manual and tosses it over his shoulder.

"Well, I'm a panda," he says at the door. "Look it up."

The waiter turns to the relevant entry in the manual and, sure enough, finds an explanation. "Panda. Large black-and-white bear-like mammal, native to China. Eats, shoots and leaves."

As this joke shows us, just one extra comma changes the entire meaning of a sentence. Consider the difference between *Eats, shoots and leaves* and *Eats shoots and leaves*. Most likely, a misplaced punctuation mark in your paper will not result in the firing of any guns; however, a number of misplaced punctuation marks or stylistic errors may result in a B+ rather than an A. This is because grammar is not just a series of unfortunate rules that you are supposed to learn. Rather, grammar is what enables us to communicate effectively.

APA Style Simplified: Writing in Psychology, Education, Nursing, and Sociology,
First Edition. Bernard C. Beins.
© 2012 John Wiley & Sons, Inc. Published 2012 by John Wiley & Sons, Inc.

In this chapter you will read about good grammar and elements of style. If grammar symbolizes the tools of construction, then style symbolizes the way you decorate that construction.

Recognizing the Importance of Good Grammar and Style

Generally, grammar and style do not seem to be exciting topics. They involve rules that don't make sense (e.g., why is it considered improper to end a sentence with a preposition?) and seemingly obscure terms that confuse more than they clarify. Furthermore, knowing the difference between a subordinating and a correlative conjunction does not necessarily mean that a writer is able to use them correctly (the latter connects two independent clauses in a particular way and the former joins an independent clause with a dependent one).

Communication, however, does not occur only at the level of grammar. Through your style of writing, your words also convey a specific tone that carries beyond the denotative meaning. Consider that the way you describe your research paper to a friend and to your psychology professor would probably be different. Academic tone tends to be more formal than that of daily conversation. To write in a way that conveys such a tone avoid the following:

- contractions (use *do not* rather than *don't*);
- colloquial expressions, such as *you know* and *got to*;
- vague expressions, such as *practically all*, *most of them*, *a lot*, *some*;
- shortcuts used for instant messaging or text messaging such as *lol* or *omg*;
- hyperbolic language, such as *stupid*, *dumb*, *awesome*, *shocking*;
- ridiculing another person's work.

Another facet of grammar and style relates to APA guidelines. APA has a citation style that differs from what scholars in the English department would use; and APA style has specific rules, such as those relating to the use of acronyms and formatting a paper.

As you can see, grammar and style are shaped by both the requirements for basic meaningful communication and the specific expectations of your readers. In other words, your writing should be stylistically fluent and technically proficient. Errors in grammar can make your reader expend a lot of effort trying to understand the meaning of a sentence, and deviations from the conventional style can weaken your credibility as a writer.

Choosing Effective Wording

Although writing in the sciences might seem dry and uncreative, there are subtle gestures you can make to increase the power and readability of your writing. For example, in addition to employing good grammar and active verbs, you can vary the kind and length of your sentences. It is not grammatically incorrect to write with a series of sentences that are the same length or with sentences that begin in the same way, but this style of writing can be tedious to read. Furthermore, if you present your information in an unvarying manner, it can be easy for your reader to overlook important information. Therefore, changing sentence length is a tool to guide your reader. Following a long sentence with a brief sentence will draw attention to the information in the brief sentence.

The way you construct a sentence also enables you to emphasize different pieces of information. Hyde (2005) wrote, "In an important experiment, Lightdale and Prentice (1994) demonstrated the importance of gender roles and social context in creating or erasing the purportedly robust gender differences in aggression" (p. 588). The examples below are phrased differently, and, as a result, highlight different information.

1. Surprisingly, the purportedly robust gender differences in aggression can be created or erased in different social contexts, according to an important experiment by Lightdale and Prentice (1994).
2. Social context is an important factor in determining levels of aggression for both men and women (Lightdale and Prentice 1994).
3. The purportedly robust gender differences in aggression need to be analyzed within their social context, as shown by Lightdale and Prentice (1994).
4. Although one may believe that gender differences are innate, Lightdale and Prentice's (1994) research demonstrates the importance of gender roles and social context in creating or erasing the purportedly robust gender differences in aggression.
5. Research by Lightdale and Prentice (1994) has shown that levels of aggression, generally thought to be higher in males, are affected by social context as well as biology.

The way you start a sentence can give your reader clues about how to read the sentence and to connect it to other ideas. Words like *surprisingly* and *although* signal a relation between ideas that may be one of contrast (examples 1 and 4). Also, note that example 2 mentions the researchers only in a citation, whereas the original sentence and examples 1 and 5 emphasize the role of the researchers. Lastly, compare the tone of sentences 2 and 3. Sentence 2 offers information in a relatively neutral tone, whereas sentence 3 expresses a more persuasive tone with the word *purportedly* and the phrase *need to be*.

Another aspect of effective wording involves the skillful use of transitions that show a relation among ideas or concepts in your writing. Transitions bridge ideas, signaling the kind of statement you are making. Table 2.1

Table 2.1 Transitions and Their Uses

Purpose	*Transition words*
To add	accordingly, in addition, both … and, equally important, further, furthermore, moreover, not only … but also
To show contrast	although, but, in contrast, conversely, despite, meanwhile, on the other hand, notwithstanding, otherwise, rather, whereas, yet
To show similarity	in the same way, likewise, similarly
To show exception	despite, however, in spite of, nevertheless, still, yet
To show that you are elaborating on a point	that is, in fact, to illustrate, in other words
To show a result	because, as a consequence, consequently, hence, for this (these) reason(s), as a result, therefore, thus
To show the passage of time or sequence	after, afterward, at this point, before, concurrently, earlier, finally, following, formerly, immediately, meanwhile, next, previously, prior to, simultaneously, subsequently, then, thereafter, thus, while, since
To give an example	to demonstrate, for example, for instance, in another case, to illustrate, in particular, in this case, in this situation, specifically, such as
To emphasize	actually, certainly, extremely, emphatically, in fact, indeed, most importantly, unquestionably, without a doubt, without reservation
To summarize or conclude	as I have shown, in brief, to conclude, in conclusion, hence, on the whole

offers a series of situations in which you might use transitions as well as a list of transition words or phrases you can use to illustrate a relation. Transitional words and phrases in each row can take on slightly different meanings. Thus, it is important that you use transitions deliberately.

Using Inclusive and Appropriate Language

Inclusive language means language that does not unnecessarily exclude or single out groups of people. We emphasize inclusive language because of concerns about precision and ethics.

Regarding precision, good research requires accuracy. Accuracy is critical not only to the validity of your results, but also to your credibility as a researcher. If your pool of participants includes men and women, using masculine pronouns (*him*, *his*, or *he*) to refer to an average participant is a form of exclusive language and does not accurately reflect your research.

Exclusive language pertains also to the ethical representation of those who have participated in, and are affected by, your research. For example, words such as *man* (the noun and the verb *to man*), *mankind*, and *man-made* have been used instead of *people*, *humankind*, and *synthetic* or *manufactured*. Although you may think masculine words refer to or include all people, the exclusion of women from this kind of language is based on sexist assumptions that men *could* stand for all people or that men are the *only* people who manufacture products. Consider that in the United States women have traditionally had lower status than men in just about all areas of life. For example, women have been able to vote for fewer than 100 years and for a long time could not own property. Therefore, using *man* to represent men and women reproduces a culture of sexism and gender inequality, even if you do not intend to do so.

Appropriate and accurate writing practices also consist of avoiding language that might be offensive to participants and to readers, or that might unnecessarily single out a group of people. For example, the phrases *female doctor* or *Black scientist* single out women and Black people. Unless gender or racial identity is important to your research, using those phrases may imply that *doctor* means *male doctor* and *scientist* means *White scientist*.

If you do need to describe a person's identity characteristics (gender, race, sexuality, ethnicity, religion, etc.) be sure that you name only those characteristics that are relevant to the topic about which you are writing.

If all your participants are male, then it is not exclusive to write *The rise in blood pressure for a participant correlates with his level of stress*. Nor do we suggest that you merely replace masculine language with feminine language. *The rise in blood pressure for a participant correlates with* her *level of stress* is not more inclusive if your participants include men and women.

Below are some suggestions for revising prose that contains gender-based exclusionary language or language that may be inappropriate.

- Inappropriate: The rise in blood pressure for a participant correlates with his level of stress.
- Appropriate:
  - The rise in blood pressure for a participant correlates with his or her level of stress.
  - The rise in blood pressure for all participants correlates with levels of stress.
  - The rise in blood pressure for all participants correlates with their levels of stress.
  - A rise in blood pressure correlates with one's level of stress.
- Instead of *chairman*, *layman*, and *fireman* use *chair*, *layperson*, and *firefighter*.
- Use parallel nouns. For example, instead of *man* and *wife* use *husband* and *wife*.
- Be aware of how you label groups of people. Decisions may not be easy, though, because labels continue to evolve. You might consult published research or sections 3.11–3.17 in the APA *Publication Manual* to find what other authors have used and what the conventions of the field are.
- Use identity labels only when they are an integral part of your research.

Deciding on the Use of Technical Language

As noted throughout this book, the kind of language you choose should be appropriate for those who will be reading your writing. If your reader needs to look up a number of words or concepts in order to understand your ideas, then your writing is probably too obscure. If you devote too much space to defining concepts that are already familiar to your readers, then you may end up sacrificing the development and support of your argument. Consequently, it is important that you use technical language as you use grammar—as a tool to more clearly convey information to your reader.

The purpose of technical language is twofold: It serves as a kind of shortcut and it reflects your proficiency with discipline-related concepts. Because you use technical language to avoid explaining at length some aspect related to your work, it is a shortcut. Consider the following sentence: "The scale assessed satisfaction with amount of time spent together, communication, sexual activity, agreement on financial matters, and similarity of interests, lifestyle and temperament on a 4-point Likert-type scale" (Gallo, Troxel, Matthews, & Kuller, 2003, p. 455). The sentence refers to "a 4-point Likert-type scale" without offering further explanation of what a Likert-type scale is. *Health Psychology*, where this article appeared, is a scholarly publication, so the authors can legitimately assume that their readers already know what a 4-point Likert-type scale is.

Using technical language without knowing exactly what it means can weaken your argument. There is a greater chance that you will apply the term(s) incorrectly, and if it appears to your audience that you do not understand part of your writing topic, a reader may assume that other parts of your thesis are flawed as well. Technical language does not replace critical thinking or grammatical clarity.

Avoiding Common Problems

Apostrophe Use

Apostrophes have two primary grammatical functions: to indicate possession without the use of "of" and to indicate a contraction. Table 2.2 lists the different rules for using apostrophes to indicate possession, and how these rules may be applied correctly and incorrectly.

Although APA style discourages the use of contractions, it is better to use a contraction correctly than to incorrectly use a word that should be a contraction. Table 2.3 lists some contractions that are commonly misused.

Pronoun Use

A pronoun is a word that replaces a noun. It is important to use pronouns carefully. Below are two basic guidelines for pronoun use.

Table 2.2 Apostrophe Dos and Don'ts When Indicating Possession

Rule	Correct usage	Incorrect usage
Add 's to the end of the word if the word is in singular form, even if the word ends in the letter *s*.	the rat's behavior, James's discussion	the rats' behavior, Jame's discussion, James' discussion
Add 's to the plural form of a word if the word does not end in the letter *s*.	the children's expectations, the mice's brains	the childrens' expectations, the mices' brains
Add an apostrophe to the end of a plural noun that ends in the letter *s*.	the subjects' responses, the students' musical training	the subject's responses, the student's musical training
To attribute joint ownership, follow the above apostrophe rules, but add an apostrophe only to the last noun.	Thomas and Blackmun's experiment (this indicates that Thomas and Blackmun worked together to develop the experiment)	Thomas's and Blackmun's experiment
If you want to show possession without joint ownership, each noun needs to be given an apostrophe according to the above rules.	Thomas's and Blackmun's experiments (this indicates that Thomas and Blackmun conducted different experiments separately; note that experiments is plural)	Thomas and Blackmun's experiments
Do not add an apostrophe to the end of possessive pronouns.	yours, hers, its	your's, her's, it's or yours', hers', its'

- The pronoun must agree with the noun or nouns to which it refers (the pronoun's *antecedent*). By *agreement*, we mean that a pronoun needs to be singular or plural, depending on whether it replaces something that is singular or plural.
- It must be clear to the reader which noun or nouns the pronoun replaces, or what the pronoun's antecedent is.

Inclusive language can make pronoun–noun agreement more complicated. Often, to avoid using a masculine pronoun to refer to all people,

Table 2.3 Frequently Misused Contractions

Contraction	Uncontracted form	Similar word	Meaning of the similar word
you're	you are	your	Belonging to you
it's	it is	its	Belonging to it
they're	they are	their	Belonging to them
they're	they are	there	indicates location/ where something is

Table 2.4 Pronouns and Agreement in Number

Sample sentence	Agreement in number	Reference to the antecedent
Everyone should do their homework.	*Everyone* is a singular pronoun, and *their* is a plural pronoun. Therefore, the pronoun and its antecedent do not agree.	*Their* can refer only to *everyone*. Therefore, *their* has a clear antecedent.

Possible revisions
Everyone should do his or her homework.
Everyone should do homework.
You should do your homework.
All students should do their homework.

a writer may use a pronoun that does not agree with the noun it replaces. Table 2.4 offers a sentence with pronoun misuse related to inclusive language.

If you are not sure if a pronoun is singular or plural, use the pronoun in a sentence with the verb *is* or *are*. The pronouns *everybody* and *they* both could refer to more than one person. However, you would write *everybody is happy* rather than *everybody are happy*, indicating that *everybody* is a singular pronoun. On the other hand, you would write *they are happy*, not *they is happy*, which shows you that *they* is a plural pronoun.

In addition to agreement in number, clarity of reference is important when using pronouns. The meaning of a sentence might be clear to you as

Table 2.5   Pronouns and Antecedent References

Sample sentence	Agreement in number	Reference to the antecedent
We think that beliefs shape religious people's decision-making processes; therefore, we examine them in this study.	*Beliefs* and *people* are plural nouns. *Them* is a plural pronoun, so there is not an error in agreement.	*Them* could refer either to *beliefs* or to *people.* Therefore, *them* has an unclear antecedent

Possible revisions
We think that beliefs shape religious people's decision-making processes; therefore we examine beliefs about an afterlife in this study.
In this study we examine how beliefs shape a religious person's decision-making process.

a writer; however, for a reader pronouns can make meaning ambiguous. Table 2.5 offers an example of a pronoun-related problem and a solution.

Verb Forms

For clarity and brevity use the active voice when possible and use the passive voice only when necessary. Sentences written in an *active voice* have an *active verb*, or a verb whose subject is doing the action. For example, in the sentence *The participants answered 10 questions*, the verb is *answered* and the subject is *participants*, and it is the participants who are doing the action. In the sentence *The 10 questions were answered by the participants*, the subject becomes *10 questions*, and the verb *were answered* is passive. For more examples, see Table 2.6.

In addition, your writing will be more compelling if you to limit your use of forms of the verb *to be* (e.g., *is, are, am, was, were*). Compare the following two sentences:

1.   There is a lot we can learn from this research.
2.   We can learn a lot from this research.

Both sentences are grammatically correct, yet, *there is* in the first sentence adds words needlessly. Besides ease of reading, an advantage of avoiding forms of *to be* is that your prose is crisper and more dynamic.

Table 2.6   Active and Passive Verbs

Sample sentence	*Analysis*
The social-cognitive observational learning model suggests that normative beliefs about aggression, hostile biases about the world, and aggressive social scripts are all learned from observing violence. (Huesmann, Moise-Titus, Podolski, & Eron, 2003, p. 217)	It is clear that the subject is *model* and the verb is *suggests*
That normative beliefs about aggression, hostile biases about the world, and aggressive social scripts are all learned from observing violence is suggested by the social-cognitive observational learning model.	The subject is *beliefs* and the verb is *is suggested*. This passive voice construction makes the reader work harder to find the verb and is more wordy than the active voice construction.
It has been suggested that normative beliefs about aggression, hostile biases about the world, and aggressive social scripts are all learned from observing violence.	The verb is *has been suggested*, but because the subject is *it* we do not know who is doing the suggesting. Passive voice constructions allow you to omit the agent of the verb, so your sentence may be less precise and more confusing.

Spelling

As a language, English has borrowed from many other languages, so rules of spelling are sometimes inconsistent from one word to another. The rules in Table 2.7 will give you a good sense of how to deal with many words that you are likely to use, but when you are in doubt, you can consult a good, college-level dictionary for further information.

Specific Word Use

In APA style, there are some rules regarding specific word use. Although these rules may not pertain only to APA style, they are considered important enough (and are violated enough) that the *Publication Manual* singles them out for special attention. These rules appear in Table 2.8.

Table 2.7   Rules for Forming Plurals

Rule	Examples
Nouns ending in *is* often form plurals by changing the *i* to an *e*.	Correct: *hypothesis* becomes *hypotheses*. Incorrect: hypothesises Examples following this rule: *hypothesis, thesis, crisis, diagnosis*
Nouns ending in *us* often form a plural by changing the *us* to *i*.	Correct: *stimulus* becomes *stimuli*. Examples following this rule: *focus, fungus, nucleus, syllabus*
Nouns ending in *on* may form plurals by changing *on* to *a*. This holds true for nouns that come from Latin or Greek, but not for nouns that come from English, such as *coupon*, which form plurals simply by adding *s*.	Correct: *phenomenon* becomes *phenomena*. Examples following this rule: *phenomenon, criterion* Note: Traditionally, the plurals of foreign words such as *schema* and *stigma* were formed by adding *ta*, as in *schemata* and *stigmata*. It is common now to see such plurals as *schemas* and *stigmas*.
Some nouns have the same form in singular and plural.	Examples following this rule: *species, sheep, fish*
Some nouns have a plural form but take a singular verb.	Examples following this rule: *news, linguistics, athletics* Note: *Statistics* as a discipline is singular; as an *application*, statistics is plural. Examples: *Statistics is a quantitative discipline*, but *In this research, the relevant statistics are the mean, median, and mode.*
Compound nouns may form plurals by making the initial noun plural.	Correct: *mother-in-law* becomes *mothers-in-law*. Incorrect: mothers-in-laws Examples following this rule: *attorneys general, passers-by*
Words that end in *ex* used to form plurals by changing the *ex* to *ices*, but the current form is simply to add *es*.	Correct: *index* becomes *indexes* (rather than the old-fashioned *indices*)

Words from Latin and Greek retain their original forms in the plural.	Correct: *datum* becomes *data*. Note: Never use *data* or *media* as singular nouns; instead use *datum* or *medium*. Examples following this rule: *datum* becomes *data*, *medium* becomes *media*, *alumnus* becomes *alumni*, *alumna* becomes *alumnae*. Note: In classical Latin, *alumni* and *alumnae* were pronounced identically, with a long *i* at the end. So in speech, they were not differentiated. Most speakers now would pronounce them differently. With the current attempt to avoid language that some might consider sexist, writers often use genderless terms such as *graduates* or *alums*.
Words that end in *o* often form plurals by adding *es* after the *o*, although words associated with music often do not.	Correct: *motto* becomes *mottoes*, *cello* becomes *cellos*. Examples following the *es* rule: *hero* (*heroes*), *memo*, *potato* Examples following the *s* rule: *cello* (*cellos*), *radio*, *stereo*, *quarto* Note: There are many exceptions (e.g., *typos*, *albinos*, *tacos*) to rules about forming the plural, so unless you are absolutely certain about the form of the plural, look it up in the dictionary.
Collective nouns are sometimes used as singular nouns and sometimes as plural nouns.	When the group referred to acts as a unit, the noun is singular. Example: *The faculty is on strike.* When the people constituting the group are acting as individuals, the noun is plural. Example: *The faculty are going home after their meeting.* Note: Words and phrases such as *a lot* and *a number* are often plural in meaning, so it is appropriate to write *A number of people are on the street* even though the subject of the sentence is *number*, which usually takes a singular verb such as *is* rather than the plural *are*.

(Continued)

Table 2.7 *(cont'd)*

Rule	Examples
In extremely rare situations, it is appropriate to use an apostrophe to form a plural.	Sometimes people may use an apostrophe to form the plural of a letter of the alphabet or a number if including the apostrophe would prevent ambiguity. Regardless of whether you use an apostrophe, write the letter or the number in italics and add the letter *s* not in italics. Example: *A's* are hard grades to earn in classes. By not using the apostrophe, a reader could think you were using the word *as*.
Words that end in *s* or *s*-like sounds form plurals by adding *es*.	Correct: *hex* becomes *hexes*. Incorrect: hex's, hexs Examples following this rule: *sex* (used as a noun), *scratch, kiss*
Nouns and verbs ending in *y* form plurals by using *ies*.	Correct: *try* becomes *tries*, *penny* becomes *pennies*. Incorrect: penny's Examples following this rule: *penny, baby, cry* Note: Do not change the *y* to *ies* for family names like *Kelly*, which would be *Kellys* in the plural, or for nouns with a vowel before the *y* (e.g., *day* becomes *days*).

Table 2.8 Specific Word Use in APA Style

Word	Guideline
that and *which*	*That* is appropriate for restrictive clauses that are necessary for the meaning of a sentence. Example: *The word that was in the wrong place changed the meaning of the sentence.* *Which* is appropriate for nonrestrictive clauses that merely provide more information. Example: *The participant identified the word, which was partially obscured.*
who and *that*	*Who* refers to people, whereas *that* generally refers to nonhuman animals, objects, or ideas. Example: *The dog that was barking frightened the girl who entered the yard.*
while and *although*	*While* is a temporal conjunction, so use it only when referring to time. Example: *He ate an apple while he waited* versus *Although he made a mistake, he was able to recover.* (Not *While he made a mistake …*)
since and *because*	*Since* is a temporal conjunction, so use it only when referring to time. Example: *He has not eaten since breakfast* versus *She was angry because he insulted her.* (Not *… since he insulted her*).
using the subjunctive mood	Actions that did not occur or that are improbable take subjunctive verbs, which look like plural, past tense verbs. Examples: *If 1 were 12 years old again, I would do things differently* and *If she were prepared for the test, she would have passed it.*
between and *among*	*Between* is appropriate when discussing two things, whereas *among* is appropriate for three or more things. Example: *The poet had to decide between love and hate as a theme of her work* and *The poet had to decide among love, hate, and death as a theme of her work.*
sex and *gender*	In APA style, *sex* refers to biology, but *gender* refers to cultural considerations.

(Continued)

Table 2.8 (cont'd)

Word	Guideline
female/male and *woman/man* or *girl/boy*	Example: *Estrogen is present in the bodies of people of both sexes* and *Promotion to executive positions in corporations does not occur equally in both genders.* Note: In some disciplines, scholars do not accept this usage.
	In APA style, *female* and *male* are usually adjectives, whereas *woman, man, boy,* and *girl* are nouns. Example: *People expect stereotypically female behaviors from girls and women.* Exception: If the age range of people being discussed is considerable, the general words female and male may be used as nouns.
Black and *White*	When referring to people of African descent as *Black* capitalize the word; similarly, when referring to people of European descent as *White,* capitalize the word. All words designating racial or ethnic groups are capitalized.
Black or *African-American, Native American* or *Indian, Asian* or *Oriental*	Social norms change, but current conventions are such that *Black* or *African-American, Native American* or *Indian* are considered acceptable. People of Asian descent should be called *Asian* (or a more specific, appropriate term, such as *Laotian*); the term *Oriental* is considered pejorative and should not be used to label people or groups. *Oriental* is acceptable as an adjective describing objects, such as an *Oriental carpet.* APA style specifies that, ideally, researchers should describe people as those people wish to be described.
sexual preference and *sexual orientation*	In APA style, *sexual orientation* is preferred over *sexual preference* unless you are explicitly talking about a person's choice. *Gay* is appropriate as a generic term used to describe people, although some might consider it sexist because it is a general term used to describe men. If there is any ambiguity in meaning, use the term *gay men.* The appropriate term for gay women is *lesbian.* The term *homosexual* is not considered appropriate because it has been used in a generally negative sense in the past.
disability and *handicap*	Avoid referring to people as being synonymous with challenges they face, such as referring to them as *schizophrenics* or *anorexics.* Instead, refer to them using wording such as *people with schizophrenia.* Use *handicap* to refer to physical limitations, such as being handicapped by lighting that is too dim, curbs that are too high, and so forth.

If you have further questions about spelling (or definitions), the following links will take you to useful online dictionaries:

- http://www.m-w.com/
- http://www.websters-online-dictionary.org/
- http://dictionary.reference.com/

3

The Introduction Section

One good paragraph at the very start, indeed, accomplishes all sorts of magic.

Katherine Frost Bruner

Writing your Introduction is simple. All you have to do is answer the following questions: What are you doing? What do we already know about the topic? Why is it interesting, and how will it advance our knowledge? What do you expect to happen and why?

When you have answered these questions, you have finished your Introduction. This chapter will help you organize the Introduction section of your APA-style research paper so that you will have addressed the questions above. After finishing this section, your reader will be able to understand how your ideas developed and what sources contributed to them. In subsequent chapters, you will see how you can develop the other sections of your research paper.

The introductory section provides a blueprint for the ideas you are developing in your paper. Your job in this section is to (a) identify your topic (i.e., what are you doing?), (b) discuss what psychologists already know and what questions remain to be answered, (c) explain how your research will fill in some gaps in our knowledge (i.e., why are you doing it?), and (d) provide the logic of your hypotheses (i.e., what do you expect to happen and why do you think this?) You should try to accomplish these goals while engaging the reader with clear and cogent writing (i.e., your writing should

APA Style Simplified: Writing in Psychology, Education, Nursing, and Sociology, First Edition. Bernard C. Beins.
© 2012 John Wiley & Sons, Inc. Published 2012 by John Wiley & Sons, Inc.

be interesting). One of the most difficult aspects of writing the Introduction is to offer enough detail for readers to develop a good grasp of the material without distracting them with irrelevant information.

Introducing the Topic

Your manuscript begins with the title of the paper at the top of the page immediately following the Abstract. One feature of APA style is that you do not type the word *Introduction* (or your name, as author) to begin this section. According to the *Publication Manual,* the Introduction section does not need a label because, by virtue of its position, the reader will recognize that it is the introductory material.

Authors typically structure the Introduction section so that broad, more general, ideas appear first, with details specific to the author's research coming later. Writers can capture the reader's interest by starting the Introduction in any number of ways. You will be more successful in engaging your reader if you begin with a compelling and original opening statement; you will be less successful if you make an uninspired statement. For instance, suppose you want to study people's sense of humor. You might begin your Introduction in one of the ways given below.

- Just about everybody claims to have an above-average sense of humor. This is an impossibility because, although some people possess a clear sense of humor, one can spot a great many humor-impaired people.
- Researchers have conducted many studies concerning people's sense of humor. The present study will investigate that trait in individuals.
- Humor is an important part of people's social lives. Consequently, psychologists have studied this trait extensively.

How effective would they be? The first example would probably be the most enticing. It states the general topic of the paper (sense of humor), and the idea of somebody being humor impaired might pique a reader's interest. The second example establishes the general topic, but it is not very interesting. The third example might not draw the reader to the topic. After reading it, he or she would know the article is about humor, but would not know exactly what aspect of the broad topic of humor; furthermore, the writing is not particularly engaging.

Different Approaches to Starting the Introduction

You will encounter some standard approaches to the Introduction section as you read journal articles. Other authors have made additional suggestions (e.g., Kendall, Silk, & Chu, 2000) about ways to begin your writing. You should select a way that fits the message you want to convey.

Citing an Actual Event

Some authors describe actual events that relate to the focus of their research. One study that reflected this approach involved people's inability to recognize their own incompetence.

> In 1995, McArthur Wheeler walked into two Pittsburgh banks and robbed them in broad daylight, with no visible attempt at disguise. He was arrested later that night, less than an hour after videotapes of him taken from surveillance cameras were broadcast on the 11 o'clock news. When police later showed him the surveillance tapes, Mr. Wheeler stared in incredulity. "But I wore the juice," he mumbled. Apparently, Mr. Wheeler was under the impression that rubbing one's face with lemon juice rendered it invisible to videotape camera. (Kruger & Dunning, 1999, p. 121)

Creating a Fictional Scenario

Another approach is to create a fictional scenario (i.e., a brief story) introducing the general point of the study. An example from a journal article exploring how people try to understand the behaviors of others illustrates this approach.

> Sylvia is a typical college student. She does, however, have persistent doubts about her ability to understand the reasons for people's behaviors. Five minutes into the first lecture of her social psychology class, a male student stands up and loudly demands to know why the class is not meeting in a different room. The professor gives a reasonable answer, but the student rejects it and stomps out of the lecture hall. Aghast, Sylvia (like the rest of the class) infers that the student is emotionally unbalanced. Several minutes later, the professor welcomes him back and introduces him as her T.A. She then explains to all that the T.A. had no choice about what kind of part to play in this class demonstration. Most of the class still perceives their T.A. to be slightly

unstable, thereby showing the correspondence bias (an overattribution of behavior to dispositional causes). Does Sylvia? Or, do her chronically accessible causal uncertainty (CU) beliefs influence how she processes the available information? We sought answers to such questions in the current research. (Weary, Vaughn, Stewart, & Edwards, 2006, p. 87)

Making a Compelling Statement About an Important Issue

Sometimes you can identify pressing issues of importance that capture your reader's interest. For example, one of the major focal issues among social workers is justice in society. So readers of social work research will probably respond well to statements about important issues of justice.

> Racial discrimination poses one of the most devastating forms of oppression in the modern era. The systematic exploitation and abuse of whole populations by other groups more powerful and different in appearance have pockmarked human history since the European mercantilist ventures of the 1500s. (Coleman, 2011, p. 91)

> Shortly after World War II, social scientists attempting to understand the atrocities of the Holocaust began searching for explanations about the catastrophic failures of humanity that had occurred during the conflict. One of their most basic discoveries was the importance and centrality of empathy in sustaining the social contract. (Gerdes, Segal, Jackson, & Mullins, 2011, p. 109)

Among educators, innovative approaches to learning are always of interest. So beginning your Introduction by describing an important current issue is likely to catch the readers' eye and capture their attention.

> There is strong evidence that computer games are hugely popular. For example, as of 2002, more money was spent on computer games in the United States—$6.9 billion—than on box-office movies, and approximately 145 million Americans (or about 60% of the population over age 6) regularly played computer games (Lee, Park, & Jin, 2006). Advocates of educational gaming have proposed that educators should harness the appeal of computer games as a vehicle for fostering student learning, but reviews of the research literature have not yielded strong support for the instructional effectiveness of computer games. (Adams, Mayer, MacNamara, Koenig, & Wainess, 2011, p. 1)

Identifying the Scope of Previous Research

In most journal articles, authors simply establish the main topic in a straightforward way, giving the reader a sense of the paper's connection to related research topics. For example, one study of college student suicide began by referring to the general nature of previous research.

> The literature on suicide, suicidality, and suicide risk factors is extensive. The research includes clinical reports, intervention strategies, identification of individual risk factors, demographic patterns of suicide and estimates of base rates in different ages and cultures. A subset of this literature has examined suicide in college students. College student suicide research is longstanding and an increasing number of articles address the topic each year. (Stephenson, Belesis, & Balliet, 2005, p. 5)

Presenting a Statistic

Another approach is to cite an interesting statistic that will engage the reader. This tactic can be successful, but you should take care not to start with statistics that will bore the reader. One research report on health and disease opened with a statistic that might capture the interest of nurses, sociologists, social workers, and psychologists who are interested in health issues.

> Health outcomes are increasingly recognized as socially patterned. In 2001–2002, the leading three causes of death in the United States were heart disease, cancer, and stroke. (Jackson, Kubzansky, & Wright, 2006, 21)

Another study focused on statistics associated with AIDS.

> Over the past three decades smoking prevalence in the general Australian population has declined.... However, this trend has not been reflected in smoking rates in the Indigenous Australian population.... Further, smoking contributes to approximately 20% of all deaths in Indigenous Australians. (Thompson, 2011, p. 90)

Citing a Quotation

Sometimes, a quotation around which an article focuses can raise a reader's interest. In the realm of education, researchers have dealt with issues repeatedly across generations, so beginning the Introduction with a quotation can put your own issue into context.

> Students ... will listen to a lecture, hearing the words and understanding their logical structure and their meaning and, as best they can, ... memorize their notes.... But the content does not become part of their own individual system of thought, enriching and widening it. ... The student and the content of the lectures remain strangers to each other, except that each student has become the owner of a collection of statements made by somebody else. (From Ku, Dittmar, & Banerjee, 2011, p. 1)

Among many people, a quotation by Sigmund Freud will generate interest. In an article on Freudian repression, Boag (2006) took advantage of such reader interest.

> Freud once wrote, *"the essence of repression lies simply in turning something away, and keeping it at a distance, from the conscious"* [italics in original]. (Boag, 2006, p. 74)

Describing Common Occurrences

Another tactic to generate interest in your ideas is to describe a common experience to which the reader can relate. A description of gender-based discrimination in hiring as the focus of an opening paragraph serves as a good example.

> For traditionally male jobs, ... women are less likely to be hired than men. They are also paid less, given less authority, and promoted less often. ... Conversely, male applicants are discriminated against for jobs that are considered feminine. (Uhlmann & Cohen, 2005, p. 474)

In composing your Introduction, you should ask yourself whether you would enjoy reading it. If you wouldn't enjoy your own writing, it is pretty certain that nobody else will. As a rule, readers are not going to be captivated by writing that begins with names of authors they don't know, and they won't care about the date an article was published (e.g., "In 1999, Dunning and Kruger found that ..."). Instead of starting with this type of mundane fact, you should try to entice your reader with your opening statement. The adage that you only get to make a first impression once certainly holds for your Introduction.

How to Begin

After establishing the opening premise, authors of a journal article are likely to include references to books, journal articles, and conference presentations. In the first part of the Introduction, there will be little detail about actual research projects. Instead, the references will be related to the overall question being addressed in the paper you are reading.

For example, in a research article about true and false confessions in the legal system (Russano, Meissner, Narchet, & Kassin, 2005), the authors began their Introduction with a very broad set of ideas:

- goal of police interrogation;
- power of a confession on jury decisions;
- value of confession in avoiding trials;
- prevalence of false confessions;
- psychological processes at work in police interrogations.

The authors addressed all of these elements in three paragraphs, citing 11 references. Two points are important here as they relate to your Introduction section. First, in a few paragraphs, you are not going to be able to include the details of the research you mention. You have to limit your presentation to the most important, global issues in that research. Second, you have to make it clear how the ideas interrelate and where they are going. You don't want to give your reader the impression that you are talking about unrelated facts and ideas, merely listing one study after another.

Reviewing the Literature

No matter how novel your research idea, it is very likely that somebody has already addressed a similar question. You can conduct systematic literature searches to identify research related to yours. Depending on your topic, you might locate many more articles that you could possibly read.

You should not try to read everything. Your literature review does not need to be absolutely exhaustive, but it should be illustrative. That is, you should read enough background material so that you can discuss the research and theory, giving a reasonably complete account of our knowledge of the topic.

Your treatment of the topic should address any controversies in the area. What are the sources of disagreement among scholars and researchers? You can use selective examples that represent what investigators have found. You might have your opinion regarding the subject you are studying, but stating your opinion is not the purpose of the Introduction. Rather, in this section you are supposed to present ideas that are based on data and theory, including conflicting views of different researchers.

You should avoid simply listing a number of studies, describing each one as if it were unrelated to the others. The task is to make it easy for the reader to understand how all of the studies interrelate.

Reasons for Reviewing the Literature

What could happen if you do not locate relevant references? One possibility is that you might plan and carry out a study that somebody has already done, maybe better than you did. There are few rewards for simple replication of an existing study (Beins, 2009, pp. 77–79).

A second reason for perusing the existing literature related to your topic is that a reader will want to know where your idea fits in with other research. Science proceeds one small step at a time; we accumulate knowledge from one project to the next. Your research is one of those small steps. Failure to cite previous research might also lead the reader to question your expertise in the area.

A third reason for becoming familiar with the research in your area is that you might spot limitations in early work that you could remedy. Every research project answers some questions but leaves other questions unanswered.

Finally, an advantage associated with a thorough literature search is that you may be able to adapt others' methodologies, their materials and apparatus, and their statistical analysis for your research. Creating a sound methodology on your own is difficult because there are many details you have to consider. It is completely legitimate to use techniques that others have developed. You just need to make sure to credit them for their ideas. Generally, you do not present great detail about methodology in the Introduction, but if methodological details are important in how you set up your study, you might want to introduce them here very briefly.

Clarifying Terms in the Research

Researchers in every discipline have developed their own language. There are terms with specific meanings to a researcher that might have a different meaning to a layperson. For instance, *schizophrenia* is a diagnostic label relating to people with inappropriate affect and behavior, but to the general public, schizophrenia often means a split personality (which a practitioner would call *dissociative identity disorder*).

Similarly, terms may not reflect the same concepts in different domains. For instance, professionals who see the abbreviation SSRI could interpret it differently from one another. Within the realm of treatment for medical disorders, those initials stand for *selective serotonin reuptake inhibitors*, whereas in studies of emotional intelligence, the initials refer to the *Schutte self-report inventory* (Schutte et al., 1998), and in sociology and social work, people might recognize it as Duke University's Social Science Research Institute.

In your Introduction, you can let your reader know how you are using important terms. Sometimes you might be discussing a relatively obscure concept that is generally known within a limited domain. Your reader might need help understanding the concept. If you are not making use of any unusual terms or definitions, you probably don't need to worry unduly that your audience will not follow your argument, but you can let your reader know about potential confusions here.

In the same vein, you can use your Introduction to discuss the operational definitions that previous researchers have used, particularly if there is disagreement among professionals about how to measure a construct. For instance, Braveman et al. (2011) noted that a discussion of health care disparities associated with gender, race or ethnicity, disability, and other social factors requires that professionals adopt a clear operational definition of disparity – what it means and what it is based on.

Introducing Your Research: Generating a Hypothesis

In many cases, your hypothesis will be based on what a theory predicts or what other researchers have discovered. Your hypothesis will carry more weight if you present a logical argument based on existing knowledge.

As an example of how to generate a hypothesis, consider how a research team studying terror management theory (TMT) introduced their ideas (Goldenberg, Pyszczynski, McCoy, Greenberg, & Solomon, 1999). They noted that TMT deals with people's feelings of mortality—that is, knowledge that we will die some day—and how we cope with those feelings. Based on previous ideas, they created this train of logic.

1. Rank (1936) posited that neurotic people are highly conscious of their mortality.
2. Eysenck (1971) speculated that neuroticism is related to discomfort with sex.
3. Becker (1973) suggested that thoughts of sex seem to be associated with thoughts of death.
4. Rank (1932) and Becker (1973) hypothesized that if the spiritual or romantic aspects of sex are emphasized, the connection to death is removed.

Based on these ideas, the research team generated a hypothesis regarding the tendency to link sex and death among people with high levels of neuroticism.

In this research, the logic of their hypothesis was clear and orderly. Previous psychologists had provided the building blocks for the hypotheses; these researchers connected the ideas.

Idea 1   People with high levels of neuroticism associate the physical act of sex and death.

Idea 2   People with high levels of neuroticism do not connect romantic or spiritual ideas of sex with death.

Hypothesis: If people with high levels of neuroticism are induced to think about the physical aspect of sex, they will mentally transform neutral stimuli into death-related responses. On the other hand, if they are primed to think about the romantic aspect of sex, they will be less likely to transform neutral stimuli into death-related responses.

This is an interesting hypothesis, but how would you go about testing it? The researchers created a clever research task in which participants completed words when given word fragments (e.g., COFF_ _). These words could be completed to create either death-related words or more neutral words. Thus, COFF_ _ could be rendered either as *coffin* or *coffee*. The researchers' hypothesis was supported. Neurotic individuals tended to form death-related words twice as often when given a prime about the physical aspect of sex than about the spiritual aspect of sex.

The researchers' study included other variables, but the example illustrates how they developed this particular hypothesis. They had reviewed the research and theoretical literature on this topic and used a logical connection between ideas as a basis to predict the outcome of their study.

Goldenberg et al.'s (1999) study in turn led to further research. Dietz, Albowicz, and Beins (2011) reasoned that humor involving sexual themes might stimulate thoughts of death in people scoring high in a test of neuroticism compared to those scoring low. On the other hand, Strick, Holland, van Baaren, and van Knippenberg, 2009) argued that humor protects people from anxiety. So sexual humor might not affect participants high in neuroticism any differently than such humor affects people low in neuroticism.

Dietz et al. presented participants with sexually themed jokes followed by word fragments that could be completed with either death-related words or neutral words. They found that sexually themed jokes led to significantly higher generation of death-related words, providing support for TMT and reducing confidence that sexual humor serves the purpose of minimizing the anxiety of high-neurotic participants.

In your research project, your hypotheses should be based on what previous research has documented, just as Goldenberg et al. used previous ideas and Dietz et al. used Goldenberg et al.'s ideas. Your hypothesis will be more credible if it follows logically from established ideas. Using intuition or hunches is not particularly helpful because people may consider the same ideas but generate very different intuitions.

Finally, you should spell out the implications of your study. In their study of TMT, Goldenberg et al. essentially said, "This is what we expect to find (i.e., their hypothesis) and this is what it will mean regarding support for terror management theory (the implication)." In your writing, you should also give the reader a preview of what it will mean if your data support your hypothesis.

At the end of your Introduction, the topic of your study should be obvious, the current state of knowledge about this topic should be apparent, your expectations should be unambiguous, and the potential impact of the study should be defined. Obviously, there is no simple formula for accomplishing all of this, but a well-constructed Introduction will contain all of these elements to some degree. Thus, the reader will know where your ideas came from and where you are going to take them.

4

The Method Section

Research is formalized curiosity. It is poking and prying with a purpose.
Zora Neal Hurston

It doesn't matter how beautiful your theory is, it doesn't matter how smart you are—if it doesn't agree with experiment, it's wrong.
Richard Feynman

Language lovers like the following sentence: Time flies like an arrow, but fruit flies like a banana. At first, the beginning and the ending don't seem to go together, but if you puzzle through it, you can get its meaning. When you write a paper, your introduction and your conclusions should go together, but your reader should not have to work hard to figure out the connection. Your Method section shows how the ideas in the beginning are linked to the ideas at the end.

This chapter will highlight the points that you should include in the description of your methodology. These points link the more general or abstract concepts in your Introduction to the specific means you used to investigate the concepts critical to your research.

The Method section provides your reader with a detailed picture of exactly what you did. It is oriented more toward technical details and much less toward the subject matter of your study, and it serves two basic functions. First, it allows readers to evaluate how well your methodology answers your research question and leads to your conclusions. Second, the description of your methodology provides other researchers with the information they need to be able to replicate your study.

APA Style Simplified: Writing in Psychology, Education, Nursing, and Sociology,
First Edition. Bernard C. Beins.
© 2012 John Wiley & Sons, Inc. Published 2012 by John Wiley & Sons, Inc.

As such, you should offer the reader sufficient detail to permit comprehension and reproduction of your research. It seems that providing such a description should be fairly easy, but, in reality, you have to make quite a number of choices about what to include and what to omit. If you give too little detail, your reader will not have sufficient knowledge to assess your study or to replicate it. If you give too much detail, you will lose your reader in boring and meaningless facts.

When you write your Method section, keep your readership in mind. You have planned and conducted your study, so you know just about everything important about it. However, what you are writing may be the first exposure that the readers have had to your topic, so concepts that are completely clear to you may be largely unknown to others. Similarly, the methodology for your study may be obvious to you because you may have tested many participants. It will not be so clear to a naive reader.

A good strategy is to regard your audience as consisting of people who are intelligent but uninformed. Your writing should call upon their intelligence as you teach them about your research.

Participants and Subjects

Human Participants

Much behavioral research entails studying college students (Plous, 1996; Thomas & Blackman, 1992). These students have some generally predictable characteristics: They tend to be young, often first-year students; White; middle class or higher, socioeconomically speaking; female; intelligent and well educated; cooperative; and responsible. However, even though most research involves people, some psychologists study nonhuman animals.

Historically, people (or indeed nonhuman animals) were referred to as *subjects*. Then, a couple of decades ago, the authors of the APA's *Publication Manual* decided that because people are actively engaged in a behavioral or cognitive research session, the term *participant* was more descriptive. Although researchers generally complied with this decision in their writing, it was not unusual to hear people speaking about *subjects*, and some people (e.g., Roediger, 2004) were quite unhappy about the new terminology.

The people at the APA must have been paying attention because the current version of the *Publication Manual* specifies that the word *subject* is appropriate (American Psychological Association, 2010). So in your writing, either *subject* or *participant* is acceptable in APA style. Your instructor may have a preference, however, and you should describe the people in your research accordingly.

The difference in designation relates to the fact that a research situation is also a social situation. Those who volunteer to take part in research interact with experimenters and have expectations about how they should act. In addition, experimenters can communicate subtle expectations. Consequently, the argument was made that people who volunteer for research are more than just subjects of study; they are active participants because they help create the dynamics of the experimental situation. When people are going about their business without knowing that a researcher is studying them, like in a purely observational study, the people are truly a subject of study. The researcher's expectations and perspectives might affect the type of observations made, but the researcher's act of observing will not affect the behavior of the person being observed.

Likewise, researchers generally believe that experimental animals do not interact with the experimenter in the same sense that humans do. The reality is that an experimenter's expectations can affect a rat's behavior (Rosenthal & Fode, 1963; Burnham, cited in Rosnow & Rosenthal, 1993). Nonetheless, it is common in APA style to refer to nonhumans as *subjects*.

Whether you intend to study people, rats, pigeons, mealworms, or some other species, it is important to inform the reader of the characteristics of those organisms. There are particular characteristics of your participants that you should communicate with your reader. Table 4.1 presents some of the general participant characteristics that you need to provide. This listing is not exhaustive, and you can tailor the information you include to meet the specific needs of your own study.

If your research question involves comparing people in different age groups, you want to emphasize the ages of people in the groups you compare. If your research entails a discussion of cultural differences, you need to tell which cultures you are studying, including enough detail about your participants so the reader is confident that your comparisons are meaningful. As the *Publication Manual* notes, even if the characteristics of your participants (e.g., sex, age, ethnicity) are not part of your data analysis, providing that information may help the reader understand the implications and limitations of your research better (American Psychological Association, 2010, p. 30).

Other information that you should report is the strategies by which you recruited your participants and the number of participants who completed the study or who dropped out. These elements can be important in

Table 4.1 Demographics of Research Participants

Characteristic	What to report
Age	*Older children, adolescents, and adults* • Average age of sample, in years • Range and/or standard deviation of age *Young children* • Age in months • Range and/or standard deviation
Sex	Number of female and male participants (man and woman, boy and girl are nouns; male and female are typically used as adjectives, although if the range of ages is considerable, APA style permits the use of male and female as nouns.)
Ethnicity	*General designations* • White • Black (or African-American) • Indian (or Native American) • Hispanic (or Latino/Latina) • Asian *Examples of subgroups if different cultures are a focus of the research* Hispanic: • Mexican-American • Mexican • Puerto Rican • Colombian Asian • Chinese • Japanese • Thai • Vietnamese • Indian
Recruitment method	*Nonprobability samples* • Convenience samples (e.g., solicitation in psychology classes) • Notices posted in public spaces, newspapers, etc. • Purposive (judgmental) sampling • Chain-referral sampling *Probability samples* • Simple random sampling (for which you specify your population) • Stratified random sampling
Inducement to participate	Extra credit in class Possibility of winning a prize in a raffle for all participants Money (including amount) No inducement

understanding your results because a random sample of people from a population may act differently from a convenience sample. For example, in studies of bulimia, samples that consist of people referred to the researchers by doctors show more severe symptoms than do samples of people suffering from bulimia in the general community (Fairburn, Welch, Norman, O'Connor, & Doll, 1996). In addition, people who are persistent enough to complete the study may be very different from those who are not. Thus, the conclusions you draw based on your research may have a lot to do with your sample.

The particular characteristics you should include will depend on the research question you are asking. Box 4.1 gives some examples of participant descriptions that require varying levels of detail. For instance, Wimer and Beins (2008) studied the effect of misleading information on participants' ratings of jokes. The intent was not to investigate cultural or social factors, so a fairly broad characteristic of participants sufficed.

On the other hand, Vorauer and Sakamoto (2006) studied formation of friendships across ethnic groups. In order for a reader to understand the nature of their research topic, the investigators provided information about ethnicity, but they did not give information about the ages of participants. Although it is common for researchers to identify the ages, Vorauer and Sakamoto simply referred to "introductory psychology students" (p. 327). The implication here is that they were traditional college-aged students, about 18–22 years old.

Sometimes, the population of participants is quite specialized and merits significant detail. This was the case for the research of Lann-Wolcott, Medvene, and Williams (2011), who studied caregivers in nursing homes and provided significant details about the people who participated in the project. Similarly, Grandey, Fisk, and Steiner (2005) investigated cultural differences in employees in the workplace. So they presented detail that far exceeds that of laboratory research, including types of jobs in which people were engaged, how long they had been employed, how many hours they worked per week, and nationality.

When research involves cultural considerations, researchers often include very detailed information about participants. For example, Abu-Bader, Tirmazi, & Ross-Sheriff, 2011) provided extensive detail about participant characteristics in their work. Their study, which is categorized as gerontological social work, involved elderly people who were members of a minority group, so issues of age, ethnicity, and length of time in the United States were all important.

Box 4.1 Participant Descriptions From Journal Articles Involving People

General Characteristics for Research That Does Not Study Social or Cultural Variables

Ninety undergraduate students are tested in this study. The participants include 61 women and 29 men whose ages ranged from 17 to 23 years ($M = 18.9$, $s = 1.2$). They volunteered in order to receive extra credit in psychology classes. (Wimer & Beins, 2008, p. 352)

More Specific Characteristics for Research That Studies Social or Cultural Variables

One hundred and twelve introductory psychology students (56 same-sex pairs) participated in the study in exchange for partial course credit. There were 22 White-White pairs, 19 White-Chinese pairs, and 15 Chinese-Chinese pairs. The ratio of male to female pairs was approximately the same across the three pair types .... Students were assigned to pairs on the basis of scheduling convenience .... (Vorauer & Sakamoto, 2006, p. 327)

Highly Specific Characteristics Required for Understanding the Research

Residents' ages ranged from 69 to 97 years ($M = 82.9$, SD $= 8.2$). Of those residents, there was one African-American male, four Caucasian males, and 15 Caucasian females. Participants' functional status was obtained using the Activities of Daily Living Scale with scores ranging from 7 to 52 ($M = 29.6$, SD $= 10.5$), with higher scores indicating greater dependency of residents on caregivers. The Minimum Data Set Cognition Scale (MDS-COGS) ranged from 4 to 9 ($M = 6.4$, SD $= 1.4$), indicating that participants were in the moderate stage of dementia (see Table 1). (Lann-Wolcott et al., 2011, p. 92)

Description of Recruitment of Participants in a Research Project

The study was conducted among staff members of 11 nursing homes of a supra-regional organization for residential elderly care located in a federal state in Germany. Participants were recruited through announcements at staff meetings and memos sent by the managers of the homes. A total of 379 out of 557 employees followed the invitation to participate in the study. Participation was voluntary, could be refused and was not motivated by any extrinsic incentives. All participants were geriatric nurses or other nursing personnel, representing 68 percent of the target group of the study. (Schmidt & Diestel, 2011, p. 317)

Participants in the study were recruited from four mosques and Islamic centers in the Washington DC metropolitan area (Washington, Maryland, and northern Virginia). The sample comprised 70 participants; 44 were men (70%), 56 were married (81%), 31 were Asians (44%), and 28 had graduate degrees (40%). Their ages ranged between 50 and 92 with a mean age of 63 years (SD = 10.2). They had been in the US between 5 and 53 years with a mean of 26 years (SD = 10.6). They self-identified as elderly. Table 1 describes the sample characteristics in more detail. (Abu-Bader, Tirmazi, & Ross-Sheriff, 2011, p. 433)

Sometimes, it can be important to be aware of specific characteristics of participants. In educational research, for instance, ages of participants can be important. Also, if there are cultural components to the research, it is a good idea to present the ethnicity or country of origin of people involved in the study.

A total of 577 teenagers from four different schools participated in the study. There were 132 Year 9 pupils from the United Kingdom (mean age = 13.87 years, SD = 0.34 years; 75 girls) and 189 from Hong Kong (mean age = 13.96 years, SD = 0.70 years; 77 girls), 125 teenagers attending Year 12 in the United Kingdom (mean age = 16.94 years, SD = 0.50 years; 68 girls), and 131 in Hong Kong (mean age = 17.47 years, SD = 0.65 years; 73 girls). (Ku, Dittmar, & Banerjee, 2011)

Another element of describing participants involves their motivation for participating. Sometimes, people receive money for participation in research; sometimes, they simply do it because they think it is a valuable activity in and of itself. Schmidt and Diestel (2011) investigated the strains and job demands of nurses by using a questionnaire. In addition to the characteristics of people in their sample, they provided information about recruitment and participation.

You should include participant characteristics that relate to your research hypotheses. If you are studying visual memory, you should include characteristics such as age, sex, education level, whether your participants have a background in visual arts, any visual impairments, and so on; in most studies of this type, it is probably not critical to indicate cultural backgrounds of your participants. On the other hand, if you are studying cross-cultural issues, ethnicity would be a critical variable to report. The information that appears in journal articles that you read can provide guidance.

Confidentiality of Participants

In your description of research participants you are supposed to provide detailed information. But, in virtually any project you complete, you need to keep participant identities anonymous and confidential. Data are anonymous when nobody can link a particular piece of data to a single individual; data are confidential when nobody outside the research project has access to information that could link participants to the study or to their data. When you present participant information in the Method section, you are legally and ethically bound not to divulge details that will reveal the identities of your participants.

Most psychological research is benign, but some studies do pose risks. You must observe extra caution if your research involves sensitive issues. Revealing behaviors of participants in such research to people who are not part of the research project would be unethical.

Nonhuman Subjects

In some medical and some psychological research, projects may involve nonhuman animals. In such research, you identify the animals in the subsection of the Method labeled *Subjects*. You need to specify the type of organism (genus and species), the age, where you obtained them, and their physiological condition.

Behavior that holds true for one species may not generalize to another, although sometimes you can predict behaviors from one type of animal to another. For instance, in some cases, nonhuman animals such as cockroaches make decisions like humans (Warren, 1965). But you cannot count on such generalizability. The fact that behaviors across species may or may not be similar in a given environment necessitates that you offer information on the species you used.

Some examples of how researchers have described the animals they have used in their studies appear in Box 4.2. As you can see, the authors have presented considerable detail about the animals.

Attrition

Sometimes the humans or animals you are studying do not finish your study, particularly in projects involving repeated testing sessions. People may not return; in some studies involving patients, they may leave a hospital or they may have died. Animals similarly may become ill or die. You should report the attrition rate in the Method section and speculate in the Discussion section how it might have affected your data.

Box 4.2　Examples of Descriptions of Subjects in Research Involving Nonhuman Animals

Rats

Male Wistar rats from Pasteur Institute (Iran), weighing 180–230 g at the time of surgery, were used. The animals were housed four per cage, in a room under a 12 hr light–12 hr dark cycle (lights on 07:00 h) and controlled temperature (23 ± 1°C). Animals had access to food and water *ad libitum* and were allowed to adapt to the laboratory conditions for at least 1 week before surgery. Rats were handled about 3 min each day prior to behavioral testing. All experiments were performed between 9:00 and 13:00 hr and each rat was tested only once. Eight animals were used in each group of experiments. (Jafari-Sabet, 2006, p. 121)

Monkeys

We studied 32 mated, but nonbreeding, adult cottontop tamarins from a captive colony at the University of Wisconsin-Madison Psychology Department. We housed all colony animals socially throughout their lives, either in family groups or in mated pairs. The tamarins ranged in age from 1 to 6 years old and had all been paired for at least 6 months prior to the beginning of the study. Tamarin pairs live in cages measuring 160 × 93 × 263 cm, furnished with natural tree branches, ropes, acrylic or polycarbonate sheeted nestboxes and various toys for environmental enrichment. We fed the colony three times daily from food platforms at least 1 m above the floor. Water was available *ad libitum*. For further details on colony husbandry refer to Ginther et al. (2001). Testing occurred either between 10:00 and 11:30 hr, before the main feed, or between 15:00 and 16:00 hr, before a high-protein snack. (Moscovice & Snowdon, 2006, p. 935)

Pigeons

The subjects were 16 female Carneau pigeons about 1 year old, originally purchased from Palmetto Pigeon Plant. They had previously participated in another autoshaping experiment that had used different stimuli. The assignment of pigeons to groups in the present experiment was random with respect to their previous treatments. They were housed in pairs and maintained at 80% of their free-feeding weights. (Rescorla, 2006, p. 139)

The problem with attrition, sometimes called *subject mortality*, is that the subjects or participants who leave your study may be quite different from those who remain. In some cases, researchers can assess the degree of similarity between those who stay and those who leave. When those who drop out are generally similar to those who remain, the outcome of the study may not differ much from what would have occurred without attrition (e.g., LaGreca, Silverman, Vernberg, & Prinstein, 1996). Unfortunately, in many cases, researchers cannot evaluate how attrition has affected their studies. Thus, if you lose participants over the course of your research, you need to specify the attrition in detail.

Materials and Apparatus

When you conduct a study, you may need stimulus materials or other implements. If you are studying learning, your participants must have something to learn. If you survey your participants, you need a questionnaire of some kind. If you are observing people for the presence of a behavior, you will need a behavior checklist. If you are performing a surgery on a rat, you will need surgical instruments.

In preparing your manuscript, you need to tell the reader about materials (e.g., questionnaires, stimulus words) and apparatus (e.g., devices to record data, surgical implements) that you used. You do not need to detail ordinary instruments you might use, such as stopwatches and computers, beyond mentioning that you used them. For specialized or unusual equipment, you should produce a clear and complete description of what you used. For example, Kolovelonis, Goudas, and Dermitzaki (2011) use a dart-throwing task in a physical education class to assess whether progress in a task differed when students recorded their own scores. (It did.) These authors provided detailed information about the dart-throwing setting because they recognized that other educational researchers would not be familiar with their setup.

A lot of behavioral research with people involves little apparatus that merits detailed description, but materials appear in virtually all human-oriented studies. The difference in designation between materials and apparatus is that materials are often printed on paper or displayed on a computer screen. Apparatus refers to instruments used by the researcher. Another way to differentiate them is that, if you drop an apparatus, it breaks; if you drop materials, they simply scatter on the floor.

In general, if researchers are likely to be familiar with your materials and apparatus, you need only mention them. But if you created your own materials, you should give a very detailed depiction of them. If you are using relatively unknown materials or apparatus created by others, you should provide a description of them and indicate to the reader where to obtain them. If you used personality inventories or questionnaires, it is a good idea to indicate levels of reliability reported by previous researchers. Some examples of descriptions of materials from published journal articles are given in Box 4.3 and apparatus in Box 4.4. You can see the extent of the description of materials provided by AbuSeileek (2011) in educational research on learning English as a second language. The materials were not as straightforward as those used by Schatzman and McQueen (2006) and merited a very detailed presentation.

Readers often do not get as interested in this aspect of the methodology as they do in the hypotheses and theories, but knowing about the materials and apparatus can be critical in a reader's decision about whether the research is worthwhile.

Box 4.3   Examples of Details of Materials in Published Research Articles

Description of Stimulus Materials

Seven reading passages of about 400 words each were used. [Texts were listed here.] … The texts were read by a pilot study of 32 first-year first-semester students and three raters. Two of the raters were English language EFL instructors and the third was a native speaker who is a specialist in applied linguistics. Students in the pilot study and the three raters read the texts to decide difficulty level (unfamiliar words to the students), interest and text suitability. The texts were selected based on the following criteria:

1) The textbook was written by a team of six professors who are specialists in English language and applied linguistics, and it is revised regularly.
2) It has been used by students in the University of Jordan, the most prominent university in Jordan, since 1999 in general language courses, and many other universities and institutions have been using it.

3) It contained some of the words that were not known for the students in the pilot study. A total of 175 words were selected by the three raters as difficult; most of them (151) were also listed by the authors as not familiar to the students. However, some of these items were deleted because they were known by the majority of the students in the pilot study, so only 147 of them were glossed.

4) Each gloss contained a synonym of 1-word, or a definition of 2–7 words. The number of glossed vocabulary items in each category from 1–7 words was twenty-one; each of the seven reading passages contained twenty-one glossed vocabulary items, distributed on three glossed vocabulary items of each category.

5) The majority of the students in the pilot study (4.59 on a five-point Likert scale) and the raters categorized the texts as interesting. They (4.78 on a five-point Likert scale) also agreed that it is not possible to understand the texts without the glossed items as the task could not be carried out without understanding them, and (4.69 on a five-point Likert scale) additional vocabulary items do not cause comprehension difficulty for participants.

6) Each text consisted of about 400 words, a number which is suitable for beginners such as the sample of this study. (AbuSeileek, 2011, p. 1283)

Twenty line drawings of nonsense objects were randomly selected from a database of nonobjects (see Fig. 1 for examples). Ten consonant-vowel-consonant (CVC) Dutch nonwords (e.g., bap) were selected as monosyllabic novel words. Ten bisyllabic novel words were constructed by adding a second syllable to each of these monosyllables (e.g., baptoe). These items are listed in Table 1. The nonsense-object pictures were randomly assigned to the novel words. (Shatzman & McQueen, 2006, p. 373)

Description of Questionnaires

Marsh's (1990) Self-Description Questionnaire (SDQII) is designed to measure self-concept in adolescents. Three scales, each containing 10 items, were used in this study: the general school scale (academic self-concept), the general self scale (global self-esteem), and the emotional stability scale. The coefficient alpha estimate of reliability of scores on each of the SDQII scales has a median of .87 ....

To measure test anxiety, Sarason's (1972) 37-item Test Anxiety Scale (TAS), with test-retest reliability at least .80 (Spielberger, 1976) was adapted. It incorporated Sarason's later (1984) work that differentiated the TAS into four components—test-irrelevant thinking, worry, tension, and bodily reactions. (Matters & Burnett, 2003, pp. 243–244)

Box 4.4   Examples of Details of Apparatus in Published Research Articles

Many behavioral journal articles do not involve apparatus, but they do involve materials. Researchers are likely to use different types of apparatus in studies involving children and nonhuman animals, and in those involving perceptual processes. Much human-oriented research involves only materials.

Research with Humans

The dart-throwing skill was selected because it was a novel task, preventing the effect of students' previous learning experiences (Zimmerman & Kitsantas, 1997). A dartboard and three darts, with steel tip, metal barrel, and plastic shaft and flights were used. The dartboard, made from papier-mâché, had a diameter of 40 cm and consisted of ten concentric circles. The central circle had 4 cm diameter and a value of ten points and each of the succeeding nine concentric circles increased the semi-diameter by 2 cm, diminishing its value by one point respectively. To control for the effect of students' height, the dartboard was fixed on a tripod and its height was adjusted so [that] the central circle [was] at each students' eye level. (Kolovelonis et al., 2011, p. 358)

The apparatus consisted of a wooden display box (106 cm high × 101 cm wide × 35 cm deep) that was mounted 76 cm above the room floor.... Each infant sat on a parent's lap and faced an opening (41 × 95 cm) in the front of the apparatus; the opening was hidden by a curtain that was raised at the start of the trial. An experimenter introduced his or her right hand (in a yellow rubber glove) into the apparatus through a curtained window (36 × 43 cm) in the back wall. (Wang & Baillargeon, 2005, p. 545)

Research with Nonhumans

The monkeys were tested by using the Language Research Center's Computerized Test System (described in Rumbaugh, Richardson, Washburn, Savage-Rumbaugh, & Hopkins, 1989; Washburn & Rumbaugh, 1992) that consisted of a PC, a digital joystick, a color monitor, and a pellet dispenser. Monkeys could manipulate the joystick through the mesh of their home cages, producing isomorphic movements of a computer-graphic cursor on the screen. Contacting appropriate computer-generated stimuli with the cursor resulted in the delivery of a 94-mg fruit-flavored chow pellet (Bioserve, Frenchtown, NJ) by using a Gerbrands 5120 dispenser interfaced to the computer with a relay box and output board (PIO-12 and ERA-01; Keithley Instruments, Cleveland, OH). (Beran, Smith, Redford, & Washburn, 2006, p. 112)

Procedure

A thorough and detailed description of the actual behaviors of participants and of researchers is critical for complete understanding of research. The trick is to include the important material and to omit the details that are irrelevant to the outcome of the study.

You should specify the sequence of steps associated with the data collection, including what the researcher does and what the participants do. This information is likely to merge the actual procedures with the materials and apparatus because it is hard to say what the participants were doing without indicating what they were doing it with.

There are some fairly standard elements in the procedure. They include:

- variables that are manipulated and measured, including independent and dependent variables;
- any conditions or groups that you intend to compare;
- how participants are assigned to, or placed in, groups;
- the role of the researcher in the session;
- the directions that participants received;
- the activities in which the participants engaged.

In essence, you should present only detail that relates to the data you collect. So if your participants are learning something, you describe the nature of the stimuli that they are learning. The nonsense words that Shatzman and McQueen (2006) created for their research, as described in Box 4.3, might produce very different learning than actual words.

As a rule, you do not need to report verbatim the directions to the participants. A summary will suffice unless there is something unusual about the instructions. If your instructions are part of a manipulation, you might want to report exactly how you instructed the participants. You should ask yourself if somebody could conduct your research in all its important aspects from the information you provide. If the answer is no, you should provide more detail.

Finally, sometimes writers include a statement with the procedure that participants provided informed consent. When you write your own procedure section, you can determine whether to include how you obtained informed consent. Strictly speaking, it is not part of the data collection process, so you can logically argue that it does not belong in this subsection.

Table 4.2 Common Elements in the Design Subsection

Element of design subsection	Possible examples
Design	Experiment with (manipulated) variables • Quasi-experiment (measured or categorical variables) • Mixed design (experimental and quasi-experimental variables) • Correlational design • Observational study • Archival study
Variables	• Independent variables • Dependent variables • Matched variables • Extraneous or confounding variables
Assignment of participants	• Random assignment • Systematic assignment • Assignment by pre-existing characteristics (e.g., sex, age)

However, for purposes of establishing that the researcher followed ethical guidelines, writers sometimes discuss how they obtained informed consent during the study.

Design

The final, common subsection regarding methodology offers a statement of the design of your study. The reader will benefit from a clear statement of your independent variables (IVs), the groups that constitute the IVs, and your dependent variables. You also specify here whether you tested your participants more than once (repeated measures) or only once (independent measures). If your design is not yet apparent to the reader before this subsection, you have one final chance to indicate how many variables are of interest in this research and how you set up your study.

Table 4.2 identifies common elements that appear in the design subsection. The guidelines presented in this chapter are not fixed rules. If it makes more sense for your presentation to identify your variables in the Procedure subsection, you may not need to include a Design subsection. The important point is that the reader should be able to find information critical to understanding your research.

5

Communicating Statistics

If you want to inspire confidence, give plenty of statistics. It does not matter that they should be accurate, or even intelligible, as long as there [are] enough of them.

Lewis Carroll

When you can measure what you are speaking about and express it in numbers, you know something about it.

Lord Kelvin

If you can't fall asleep, you might try counting sheep. As everybody knows, numbers can put your mind into a stupor that is every bit as deep as sleep. When you are reading and you see a set of numbers, does your mind go numb? If so, you know exactly what you want to avoid in your writing. Your own numbers should support your arguments, but most of the time people are going to be more interested in the words you write.

Statistics have a reputation that, to most people, is more negative than positive. People try to avoid them because statistics involve numbers, because statistics can be hard to understand, and because statistics can be deceptive. We too often forget that, when we use them properly, statistics can be highly informative. In the end, they are merely tools that people can use well or poorly.

The problem is that too many of us are so intimidated by them that we fail to evaluate them critically. We need to remember that people use statistics just as they use words—to communicate a message. A good speaker can

APA Style Simplified: Writing in Psychology, Education, Nursing, and Sociology,
First Edition. Bernard C. Beins.
© 2012 John Wiley & Sons, Inc. Published 2012 by John Wiley & Sons, Inc.

persuade an audience with well-chosen words. Politicians are very adept at creating messages to convince us that they are looking out for our welfare. It is not the fault of the words when the politicians end up lining their own pockets at taxpayers' expense. The problem lies with the failure of people to evaluate critically what the politicians are saying.

The same dynamic occurs with statistics. If people are willing to accept statistics at face value, there is no limit to the chicanery that others can perpetrate with numbers. However, as McGrath (2011) has said, "If you think it is easy to lie with statistics, you should see how easy it is to lie without them" (p. 5).

Fortunately, when social researchers use statistics to bolster their arguments, they are generally not trying to deceive. Rather, they are using statistics as a tool to help them understand behavior and to let them generate logical and believable conclusions. After drawing their inferences, researchers then use statistics to convince others of the validity of those conclusions.

In your own work, effective communication requires that you know your audience. If you are writing for a statistically sophisticated readership, you can probably assume that people reading your material will possess the technical information necessary to understand the statistics you have used. So a complete and thorough presentation of those statistics would be entirely appropriate. On the other hand, if your audience is less sophisticated about research and statistical techniques, presenting technical jargon will probably only confuse and distract them from the message that you are trying to convey.

When you write, it may be very helpful for you to imagine what a reader will think when reading your words. This strategy is useful when you decide how you want to frame your message.

Why Do We Use Statistics?

The human sciences are empirical disciplines, so we gather information to answer our questions. Most of the time, this information goes by the name *data* and most of the time it involves numbers. If we study a large group of people (or rats, pigeons, etc.), we generate a lot of information and we have to make sense of it. The most common way of making a large amount of data comprehensible so we are not swamped with too much information is to find the average score. There are several distinct averages, each computed differently. The common averages are the mean, the median, and the mode. The most frequently used is the *mean*, which is the technical term for the score you obtain by adding all your numbers and dividing by the number of scores you added. In everyday language, most people use the word *average* to reflect the mean. Sometimes we also want to find out whether the scores are bunched together or spread apart, so we find the *standard deviation*. Together, these two statistics give us a sense of the typical score (the average) and how far from the typical score we can expect other scores to be (the standard deviation).

A second use of statistics is to allow us to evaluate the similarities and differences between groups. So if we have, say, 100 measurements from one group and 100 measurements from another group, we can compute two numbers for each group, the mean (the average score) and the standard deviation (an indicator of the spread of the scores), to find out if the two groups are similar or different. There are other ways to assess the relations among the numbers, but they all have the same goal of allowing us to put measurements in context or to create a perspective that helps us think about what they mean.

A third use of statistics is to draw inferences about whether we should believe that our numbers are reliable. That is, if we gather our data from one group of people, can we expect the same result if we repeat our research or take the same measurements from a different group of people? The purpose of these inferential statistics is to establish a level of confidence that what holds true for the groups we measured will be true for different groups as well.

If you keep these three general uses in mind when you read about statistics, you will have an easier time understanding what a writer is trying to convey. Similarly, if you make clear to your reader why you are using a particular statistic, you will be helping your reader to understand the points you are making.

What Point Are You Trying to Make?

Using numbers to make a point is not much different from using words to make the same point. In both cases, you introduce an assertion that you subsequently support with logical argument. The difference between statistics and words is that statistics involve a shorthand way of making your case.

To use one of the simplest types of statistics, the average, you are able to tell the reader what is typical. An average simply depicts what you can generally expect. To cite an average, however, hides a significant amount of background information. Specifically, when you give an average, you are relying on the reader to understand that you had a group of measurements and that you used some kind of arithmetic or numerical action to come up with a single number to represent the entire group. In addition, if you are communicating with a lay audience, you might want to point out that nobody may actually have scored precisely at the mean, even if a lot of scores might be close to it. Furthermore, there are different types of averages, so your reader should know that there are various ways to come up with the average. So when you say that "The average is X", you are only giving the final step in a sequence.

To make your point effectively, it is important not to let the reader lose sight of that point or why each statement you make relates to it. Burying readers in a bunch of numbers and symbols whose relevance they do not understand is a good way to divert their attention from your message, reducing its impact.

So how can you make sure your readers know where you are taking them? You must give them sufficient detail to allow them to assemble a complete picture. This means writing a verbal statement of your point, presenting relevant statistics, and creating a verbal statement of what the numbers mean. Presenting only the numbers poses a risk that readers will not connect them to your main point; presenting only words poses the risk that readers will not be able to evaluate the cogency of your argument.

For each statistic that you provide, you need to include four elements for the benefit of the reader.

- a statement of the point you are addressing;
- a verbal summary of your statistic;
- the numerical presentation of statistical information;
- how the numbers relate to your point.

Your language should be as simple as possible, while allowing you to make your point. Some writers, particularly beginning writers, believe that using complex terms and difficult vocabulary will lead to more credible prose. The reverse is be more likely. If readers do not understand the point you are trying to make, your writing will be entirely ineffective.

Understanding Your Numbers

Numbers, by themselves, are not particularly interesting or informative. As researchers use numbers, those numbers take on meaning only when they link to an idea. We use our statistics as tools to help us understand behavior. As such, the numbers should take second place to your ideas when you write.

So you should strive to make your prose complete and comprehensible even without the numerical information. The statistics reinforce your writing in much the same way that quotations support writing in the humanities. In both cases, the writer creates an argument and then buttresses it with numbers (in the sciences) or with quotations (in the humanities). Table 5.1 provides two examples of how the technical information complements the verbal presentation but is not necessary for understanding the ideas. Naturally, the more information you include, the greater the understanding that your reader will gain. But you should be able to communicate the main points of your research without reliance on any statistical presentation whatsoever.

Table 5.2 illustrates frequently asked questions that behavioral researchers pose in their studies and the statistical tests that are appropriate for those questions. If you ask whether the averages of different groups are comparable and if your statistical test tells you that the answer to the question is "no," you have a significant effect. Basically, *significant* means *reliable*; a significant difference means that the difference is reliable—you can count on it happening again. So *t*-tests and *F*-tests let you know if the difference between groups is likely to appear again if you do your research a second time.

Similarly, if scores are paired so that knowing something about one member of the pair helps you predict the second, there is a significant relation between the two variables. Again, significant means reliable. So if you were to conduct your study a second time, you could reasonably expect to see a similar pattern in the data.

The term *significant* is a technical term, one that psychologists would probably change if they could. It means something very different in statistics and in everyday life. The reason for this usage is that one of the most influential statisticians in history, Ronald Fisher, noted that a statistical result could *signify* something, therefore it was significant. However, that usage has not survived to the present (Salsburg, 2002). In a casual conversation, if somebody tells you a significant fact, it is probably an important fact. But if your results are significant, they may or may not be important; they are simply reliable—that is, likely to recur if you replicate your original study.

Table 5.1 Examples of Text With and Without Statistical Information
Each version should communicate the same basic information; the numbers should not be necessary for the reader to understand your message.

Statistical information included	*Statistical information excluded*
Participants rated how offensive they found a set of jokes. The average rating was highest for jokes victimizing women ($M = 3.6$), with jokes victimizing men ($M = 2.1$) and neutral jokes ($M = 2.3$) showing lower levels of perceived offensiveness. This effect was significant, $F(2, 160) = 91.782, p < .001$. (Beins et al., 2005)	Participants rated how offensive they found a set of jokes. The average rating was highest for jokes victimizing women, with jokes victimizing men and neutral jokes showing lower levels of perceived offensiveness.
Participants in the different groups expected jokes that varied in humor level. People who believed that they would read very funny jokes found the jokes the funniest ($M = 4.8$), followed by participants in the neutral, no-information condition ($M = 4.0$), and then by participants who expected very unfunny jokes, who found the jokes least funny ($M = 3.2$). When we led participants to expect either horrible jokes or hysterical jokes, the ratings did not differ significantly from the neutral group ($M = 3.5$ and 3.9, respectively), $F(4, 85) = 8.59, p < 001$. (Wimer & Beins, 2000)	Participants in the different groups expected jokes that varied in humor level. People who believed that they would read very funny jokes found the jokes the funniest, followed by participants in the neutral, no-information condition, and then by participants who expected very unfunny jokes, who found the jokes less funny. When we led participants to expect either horrible jokes or hysterical jokes, the ratings did not differ significantly from the neutral group.

As an example, if standardized aptitude test (SAT) scores increase nationwide by only a few points from one year to the next, that difference is going to be statistically significant because huge sample sizes make it easy to spot small, but reliable, differences. The difference is significant in a statistical sense, but it is not particularly significant in a real-world sense. This is why psychologists have recently started reporting a statistic called an effect size. The effect size can tell you if an experimental manipulation produces a large, medium, or small effect. The larger the effect size, the more meaningful it is in a real-world sense.

Table 5.2   Common Research Questions and the Traditional Statistical Tests
Associated With Them
Each type of test has variations that are appropriate for different circumstances.
You can refer to statistics and research methods books for details on appropriate
use of these tests.

Question	Statistical test
Do two groups have the same averages?*	*t*-test, *z*-test
Do three or more groups have the same averages?	Analysis of variance (*F*-test)
When two scores are paired, are the two scores independent? Or does knowing one score give you a clue about the other score, reflecting that the scores are dependent and related to one another?	Correlation (ρ, r, Φ)
For paired scores, if you know the score of one member of the pair, can you predict the second score at above-chance levels?	Regression analysis
If you have multiple categories into which different observations can fall, does the number of observations in each group match your expectations?	Chi-square (χ^2)

*You can use the analysis of variance with two groups, but for historical reasons,
researchers generally use the *t*-test.

Helping Readers Understand Your Statistics

A number of authors (e.g., Best, 2001, 2004; Huff, 1954; Tufte, 1983) have
perused the research literature and the popular media and have found examples of poor statistical communication. Fortunately, we do not need to be vic-
tims of poor statistics. Huff (1954) suggested that experts at statistical deception
know how to mislead people with numbers, so it would be a good idea for the
rest of us to know about these tricks. Best (2001) stressed that the cure for
the so-called "bad statistic" is a recognition that we must evaluate numbers.

One of the most effective strategies to avoid giving your reader the wrong
message with your numbers is to keep your presentation as simple as possible. As the information becomes more complicated, you need to include
more statistics, but your goal should be to minimize the likelihood that
your information will distract the reader from the point you want to make.
Tufte (1983) has coined the term *chartjunk* to describe elements that appear
in graphs that distract the reader from understanding the content in the
graph. He suggested that, if you create a figure, you should maximize the

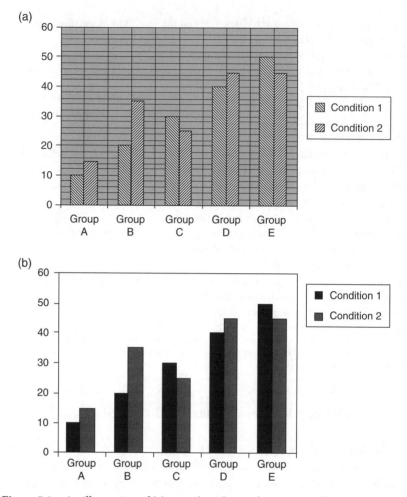

Figure 5.1 An illustration of (a) a graph with uninformative gridlines that clutter the figure and bars with a moiré effect that Tufte (1983) asserts will distract the reader, and (b) a graph with a less cluttered, more easily comprehensible format.

amount of relevant information and minimize anything that would distract the reader. For example, differentiating the bars in a bar chart or a histogram is more effective when you use darkness of shading rather than thin lines that produce a distracting, moiré effect like the one in Figure 5.1 (a).

A useful principle that Tufte identified is the maximization of the data-to-ink ratio. That is, graphs become more useful when the amount of data grows and the amount of ink decreases. Another way of saying this is that you will communicate more effectively if you present the critical information and as little else as possible in a graph.

Sometimes you can miscommunicate with words, too. Best (2001) identified what he described as "The Worst Social Statistic Ever." He pointed out that a graduate student had made the claim, based on research by the Children's Defense Fund (1994), that "[e]very year since 1950, the number of American children gunned down has doubled" (pp. 1–2). This statistic is patently impossible because if a single child had died by gunfire in 1950, the number of children in the United States felled by gunshot in the year 2000 would have exceeded one quadrillion, obviously an impossible figure. The message here is that you need to be very careful in selecting your wording. The original claim by the Children's Defense Fund about gunshot deaths was that "[t]he number of American children killed each year by guns has doubled since 1950" (Children's Defense Fund, 1994, p. x). This claim is very different from the misstatement by the graduate student. You need to ensure that your wording accurately represents the data.

Another common problem is presenting data out of context. For instance, Best (2004) pointed out that during a news broadcast in 2001, CBS anchor Dan Rather commented on the "epidemic" of school shootings after a student in California had killed two students and wounded several others. Obviously, deaths of children are tragic; multiple, violent deaths are worse. But the truth is that the rate of school-based violence had decreased by around 50% in the previous decade. Rather's comments were based on the California shooting and a few other well-publicized tragedies rather than on the mass of data that showed the schools were safer than a decade before and pretty safe compared with nonschool locations. This incident exemplifies the concept of missing data and relates to the need to understand the context in which numbers exist.

In another instance, Daniel Okrent, who worked for the *New York Times*, noted that health workers and activists had criticized the administration of President Ronald Reagan for scant funding for AIDS research. An official in the Reagan administration, Gary Bauer, asserted that AIDS funding had increased during Reagan's tenure as president. In assessing Bauer's claim, Okrent explained that AIDS had not existed as a public health issue prior to the Reagan administration, so there would have been no need for funding. Obviously, comparing contemporary funding with a time when no money was needed does not help resolve arguments. Bauer's statistics were misleading, whether or not his failure to present the whole picture was intentional (Gross & Miller, 2006).

Obviously, a few examples here cannot exhaust the ways that somebody can present a distorted message with statistics. But these examples can alert you to the need to be cautious in presenting your statistics and in assessing the statistics that others present to you.

Differentiating Results and Interpretations

When you analyze your data, the results provide a description of what has happened. You conclude that the groups you compared are significantly different or they are not. Or the relation between two variables is significant or nonsignificant. Or the number of observations in different categories matches your expectations or it does not.

If statistical results tell you what happened, it is now up to you to figure out why things occurred as they did. This is the realm of interpretation. In an APA-formatted paper, the description of what happened belongs in the Results section. The interpretation and speculation goes in the Discussion section.

Your statistics support your description of what happened. At some point, though, you need to figure out why the data emerged as they did. In your discussion, you are using your knowledge of the area, your creativity, and your insights and intuitions to speculate regarding what it all means. For just about any data set you generate, there will be more than one feasible interpretation. Your job is to generate the most plausible interpretation based on your statistics and on what previous researchers have discovered. For questions that are complex, there will always be explanations that differ from yours. Further research will resolve the issue of whether your interpretation or some other interpretation is most reasonable.

6

The Results Section

Without data, all you are is just another person with an opinion.

Unknown

Statistics may be defined as "a body of methods for making wise decisions in the face of uncertainty."

W. A. Wallis

Everybody likes a good story. An interesting plot will leave you satisfied at the end, particularly if there are surprises along the way. In the story of your research, your hypothesis is the plot, and your results provide the surprises.

In this chapter, you will learn how to present your results so the reader can see whether your data support the ideas you presented in your Introduction section. Your Results section also prepares your reader for your conclusions, which appear in the Discussion section and which is the subject of the next chapter.

You can't just make things up, though. Each element in your story should be interesting, and each provides a glimpse of the truth. In your Results section, your interesting story comes through your words; the sense and truth of your words come through your statistics.

Your ideas are the most critical aspect of the paper you are writing; the statistics are merely tools that provide support for your ideas. If you keep this relation between ideas and statistics in mind, you will find it easier to communicate with your reader.

APA Style Simplified: Writing in Psychology, Education, Nursing, and Sociology,
First Edition. Bernard C. Beins.
© 2012 John Wiley & Sons, Inc. Published 2012 by John Wiley & Sons, Inc.

Creating an outline or an idea map can be very sound because it forces you to think of your main ideas. If you have generated a reasonably complete outline or idea map, you will have a good sense of your main points and how you will support them.

Both of these approaches take a top-down approach (Salovey, 2000), which means that you are beginning with an overall sense of where your ideas are going. If you simply line up your statistics one after another, they will have as much meaning (and interest) as listings in a phone book.

You may have noticed that I have not focused very much on statistics or numbers so far. The reason is that your first responsibility in the Results section is to convey the ideas of what happened in your study. The numbers can wait. If you understand the purpose of the statistics from your data analysis, you can tell the reader in words what the numbers have revealed. The words give the idea; the numbers, which come later, support your idea and provide an element of precision to your presentation.

Your Hypothesis

In your Introduction, you will have presented your hypotheses. Normally you talk about your hypothesis in the Results section in the same order as you offered them in the Introduction. A good example of a research report that describes support for a single hypothesis involved testosterone level and aggression (Klinesmith, Kasser, & McAndrew, 2006). The investigators noted that previous researchers had discovered that insults or challenges to status can be associated with increases in testosterone levels in males. So Klinesmith et al. hypothesized that the presence of a gun (compared with a child's toy) would increase testosterone levels in men. The researchers created a task in which participants handled for 15 minutes either a child's toy or a pellet gun that resembled an automatic handgun. The investigators measured testosterone level before and after the 15-minute period. The data confirmed their hypothesis. As they reported,

> Our first hypothesis was confirmed: Subjects who interacted with the handgun showed a greater increase in testosterone from Time 1 to Time 2 than did those who interacted with the children's game. Thus, interacting with the gun increased testosterone levels. (Klinesmith et al., 2006, pp. 569–70)

This verbal presentation of the results is clear and straightforward. After reading it, you know what happened. The researchers mentioned that they tested a hypothesis, how they tested it, the pattern of results, and the fact that the data confirmed their hypothesis. You don't need statistics to understand their point.

In a research report, though, a reader expects the technical, statistical information that supports the researchers' conclusion. Here is how those researchers included the statistical information:

> Our first hypothesis was confirmed: Subjects who interacted with the handgun showed a greater increase in testosterone from Time 1 to Time 2 (mean change = 62.05 pg/ml, SD = 48.86) than did those who interacted with the children's game (mean change = 0.68 pg/ml, SD = 28.57), $t(28)$ = −4.20, p_{rep} = .99, d = 1.53. Thus, interacting with the gun increased testosterone levels. (Klinesmith et al., 2006, pp. 569–570)

As you can see, the technical information supports the verbal statement, but you don't need the statistics to understand the authors' point. When you create your own Results section, you should try to make your point using words. Then insert the technical part. This advice is a little simplistic, but as a strategy, starting with ideas instead of numbers is a good idea.

In addition, you should begin your presentation of the data with descriptive statistics. The authors who studied testosterone level presented the means and standard deviations, then the inferential statistic, a t-test.

There are numerous ways to present your data. Examples of how authors present descriptive statistics appear in Table 6.1.

Deciding What to Present

The main point of the Results section is to let the reader know what happened. Start this section with the most interesting, important, and surprising results. You should present as much detail as required in order to inform the reader adequately.

Generally, theoretical and empirical reports are meant for a readership that is versed in professional research techniques. You can expect the reader to know the difference between experimental and nonexperimental methods, the uses of various statistical tests, the norms for hypothesis and significance testing, and so forth. When you present your data and statistics, you don't need to belabor the obvious. For example, all competent researchers know that t-tests tell us whether two groups differ significantly. So don't bother explaining that fact to the reader.

Table 6.1 Examples of Presentations of Descriptive Statistics

Type of presentation	*Example*
Means in the text with standard deviations presented in parentheses	Research: Infants' reactions to sweet and bitter tasting substances The proportion of leg kicks occurring after post-tasting was similar whether the object had tasted sweet or bitter. The mean for the sweet condition was 0.584 (sd = 0.165), and for the bitter condition it was 0.604 (sd = 0.223). (From Rader & Vaughn, 2000, p. 537)
Means and standard deviations presented in parentheses	Research: Social work students' perception of field work experiences Burnout or strain-related feelings associated with the field experience were reported "rarely," using the 1 *{never)* to 7 *{always)* metric (M = 3.30, SD = .97). Similarly, satisfaction with the current field experience (M = 3.84, median = 4.0) fell closer to the "satisfied" (4) than "neither satisfied nor dissatisfied" (3) marker on the 1–5 satisfaction scale. Perceived efficacy (M = 7.67, SD = 1.46) was rated somewhat higher than an average or "fair" amount. Finally, the students rated themselves slightly more than moderately prepared (M = 5.84) on a1 *{not at all prepared)* to 10 *{extremely prepared)* scale of preparedness for entering the current field placement. (From Kanno & Koeske, 2010, p. 29)
Means referred to in the text but placed in a table (or figure)	Research: Student performance in statistics as a function of teaching emphasis As Table 1 indicates, the results show nearly equal means in the traditional-emphasis class and in both moderate-emphasis classes but notably better scores in the high-emphasis class. (From Beins, 1993, p. 162)

Unless a statistical approach is fairly obscure, you should expect the reader to know what you are talking about. Similarly, if you use standard data analysis software such as SPSS® or Minitab®, you don't need to mention it specifically.

Reporting Significant and Nonsignificant Results

Authors tend to devote space in their manuscripts to statistically significant effects and to downplay nonsignificant effects. Significant results suggest that something interesting took place, so it is not surprising for the researcher to detail it. If your data analysis reveals an unexpected, significant result, it is probably worth mentioning, but you should remember that significant effects are sometimes accidental and might not really signify anything. If you see an effect that you cannot explain, mention it, but do not develop a convoluted account of the result that is pure guesswork.

Just as researchers attend to significant effects, they minimize attention devoted to nonsignificant results. Such results let us know that something did not happen, but not why it didn't happen. Most of the time, when results are not significant, it does not pay to discuss them at great length. The problem with nonsignificance is that you don't know if the results turned out the way they did because there is no real effect or because your methodology obscured an effect that is real.

Incidentally, when your statistical analysis fails to result in a significant effect, the norm is to report it is as *nonsignificant*. Psychologists will recognize this wording in its statistical context. You should not refer to that effect as *insignificant*. If you hypothesized that there would be a significant effect and it turned out not to be, it would be *nonsignificant* statistically but it would not be *insignificant*. After all, the results differed from what you thought would happen—and that would be significant in the normal English meaning of that word.

In recent years, psychologists have recommended that researchers rely on more than merely tests of significance. Recommendations for the statistics that should appear in journal articles include effect sizes and confidence intervals (American Psychological Association, 2010; Wilkinson and Task Force on Statistical Inference, 1999). These new approaches are gradually appearing in the professional literature as investigators become more familiar with them. The nature of statistical reporting is changing, as McGrath (2011) has noted, but we do not yet know what standards will ultimately prevail. For instance, the Association for Psychological Science (APS) recommended several years ago that authors use a statistic called p_{rep}, the probability that an effect will replicate instead of the traditional p-value, but articles in APS journals no longer include this statistic.

As you write your Results section, it is probably safe to err on the side of more complete information rather than less. Thus, presenting p-values will satisfy traditionalists, and presenting effect sizes and confidence intervals will satisfy those who embrace the emerging conventions.

Marginally Significant Effects

Researchers typically adopt the Type I error rate of 5%; that is, the likelihood of mistakenly concluding that there is a real effect is 5%. For decades, authors claimed significance and rejected the null hypothesis when $p \leq .05$ and did not reject the null when $p > .05$. The analogy researchers often used involved pregnancy: you either are or you aren't. You can't be highly pregnant or slightly pregnant or nearly pregnant.

Some investigators are more comfortable with the idea that you should not ignore a possibly interesting effect, even if $p > .05$. For example, why should a p-value of .050 be so much more interesting than a p-value of .051? Further, there is no logical or scientific rationale for choosing the typical significance levels of .05 and .01; it is merely tradition. In studies with low power (i.e., small sample sizes combined with small effect sizes), it may be more reasonable to adopt significance levels of .20 or .30 (Winer, Brown, & Michels, 1991).

Authors have called potentially interesting effects that do not attain conventional levels of significance *marginally significant* when $.05 < p < .10$. Some writers (e.g., Salovey, 2000) have suggested avoiding such qualifying statements, preferring a simple statement that, for example, $p = .06$. A reader would know that such a value is not significant and can evaluate it appropriately. If you are writing about your results and an effect is not quite at the level of significance but may be important, let the reader know about it and declare that you are discussing the result with caution.

APA Style and Presentation of Your Results

APA-style presentation of results is not difficult to implement, but there are a lot of details that you have to keep in mind. The presentation style for numbers, results of statistical tests, and creation of tables and figures is quite technical. Table 6.2 gives the format for statistical presentation of commonly used tests. One notable change in APA style in the current publication manual is that authors should not routinely use the symbols for *less than* (<) or *greater than* (>) in presenting probability values. Rather, with the ubiquity of computerized data analysis, authors should present exact probability values. As the table indicates, the standard format is to present the statistical test and degrees of freedom, the computed value, the probability value, an effect size statistic, and the confidence interval for the statistic.

Table 6.2 Format for Presenting Commonly Used Inferential Statistics

Statistic	Example
Generic	*Statistic (degrees of freedom) = value of statistic, p = significance level, effect size, confidence interval [in square brackets]*
t-test[a]	$t(186) = 3.51, p < .001, d = .52$, CI [0.30, 1.06]
	$t(60) = 3.23, p = .002, d = .82$, CI [0.27, 1.15]
F-test (ANOVA)	$F(2, 33) = 5.25, p = .01$, MSE = 2.95, $\eta^2 = .24$
Correlation	$r(107) = .13, p = .18$
Chi-square[b]	$\chi^2(1, N = 46) = 1.39, p = .24$ (using the Greek letter χ)
	$X^2(1, N = 46) = 1.39, p = .24$ (using the italicized Roman letter X)

Note: APA style says that, normally, you should report test values to two decimal places; probability levels can go to three decimal places, but when a *p*-value is less than .001 (e.g., $p = .0005$), you may see it reported as $p < .001$. Also, insert a space between each element in the statistical presentation. The spaces make it easier to read.
[a] The exact probability value is appropriate unless the value to three decimal places is .000. When that occurs, use $p < .001$.
[b] When reporting a chi-square value, indicate the degrees of freedom followed by the sample size in the parentheses. You can use either the Greek letter chi (χ) or the uppercase letter X in italics.

Some common abbreviations that are standard for referring to various measurements appear in Table 6.3. In addition, standard symbols in presenting the results of statistical tests are in Table 6.4. A general rule is that if the measurement is written using Roman letters (e.g., *t*, *F*, *M*), it appears in *italics*; if the measurement is written using Greek letters (e.g., α, β, μ), it is not italicized. You may occasionally see text underlined in a typed or word-processed manuscript; underlining is the old-fashioned manner of indicating that the text should be in italics. Old typewriters were incapable of generating italics, boldface, or any other nonstandard form of print. The need to represent italics by underlining has disappeared because you can insert italics with a word processor.

Remember that the focus of the Results section is to present ideas. You are trying to convey to the reader a complete sense of what happened. If you compared two groups to see which one had the higher mean score, your first job is to tell the reader that the average score in one group is different from the average score in the other group. If you are correlating variables, you need to tell the reader that as the scores on one variable go up (or down), the scores on the second variable go up (or down). Most research

Table 6.3   Some Common Symbols and Abbreviations Used in Measurement

Symbol*	What it represents
f	Frequency
f_e	Expected frequency
H_0	Null hypothesis
H_a or H_1	Alternate or research hypothesis
M	Mean
Mdn	Median
N	Total sample size
n	Size of subsample
SD	Standard deviation
z	Standardized score
α	Probability of Type I error
β	Probability of Type II error

*Symbols appearing in Roman letters (e.g., *a*, *b*, *c*) are italicized; symbols appearing in Greek letters (e.g., α, β, γ) are not italicized. If the symbol or abbreviation has a subscript or superscript, it is not italicized.

Table 6.4   Some Common Symbols Used in Presenting the Results of Statistical Tests

Symbol*	What it represents
ANOVA	Analysis of variance
ANCOVA	Analysis of covariance
d	Cohen's measure of effect size
d'	Measure of sensitivity (psychophysics)
df	Degrees of freedom
MANOVA	Multiple analysis of variance
MS	Mean square
MSE	Mean square error
p	Probability; probability of success in binomial trial
p_{rep}	Probability that an effect will replicate
r	Pearson product-moment correlation
r^2	Coefficient of determination
r_{pb}	Point-biserial correlation
r^s	Spearman's correlation
R	Multiple correlation

Table 6.4 (*cont'd*)

Symbol*	What it represents
R^2	Square of multiple correlation
SEM	Standard error of measurement; standard error of the mean
SS	Sum of squares
t	t-test value
η^2	Eta-squared (measure of effect size)
Φ	Phi (measure of association)
χ^2	Chi-square value
ω^2	Omega squared (measure of effect size)
$^\wedge$	Caret (reflects an estimated value when used above a Greek letter)

*Symbols appearing in Roman letters (e.g., a, b, c) are italicized; symbols appearing in Greek letters (e.g., α, β, γ) are not italicized. If the symbol or abbreviation has a subscript or superscript, it is not italicized.

that you will encounter deals with those two issues: do averages differ and are variables correlated? It should not be difficult to tell that to the reader.

So what is the difficulty in presenting results? One issue is expressing the technical details in appropriate format. This is relatively easy because all you have to do is to insert them into your prose in a meaningful place and follow the prescribed format. A second issue is taking your understanding of what the numbers have told you and converting that information into coherent and comprehensible English. This requires more thought.

Creating Tables

Tables are an effective way to present a lot of information in a small space. When you have many data, it might be difficult to include them all in the text without overwhelming or boring the reader. The most difficult part of creating tables is generating a format that makes the purpose of your data transparent—that is, clear and accessible.

The first task here is to decide whether you need a table (or a figure) for your results. If you are comparing two or three groups, you would not use a table because the table would take up too much space relative to the information you are presenting. Previous editions of the APA *Publication Manual* (American Psychological Association, 2001) pointed out that tables and figures were expensive because a person had to take extra time to format it so that it would fit into a journal article appropriately. Thus, authors were cautioned to use tables only when there was a lot of information, as with research involving multiple variables that, if presented in prose format, would constitute a string of numbers that were hard for the reader to process. The most recent version of the publication manual (American Psychological Association, 2010) takes a more liberal attitude toward using tables and figures. The basic guidelines for the use of tables and figures are as follows:

Use a sentence with three numbers or fewer.
Use a table for four to 20 numbers.
Use a graph for more than 20 numbers.

As an example, consider research in which my students and I collected data about the way that women and men respond to offensive jokes that victimized either women, men, or neither gender in particular. After analyzing the results, we would communicate which groups differed in their ratings of the jokes. As such, we could (but should not) indicate the mean ratings on a scale of 1 (*not funny*) to 7 (*very funny*) using the following dense, text-dependent passage:

There was a significant interaction between sex of joke victim and sex of rater. Women rated male-victimizing jokes as funniest ($M = 3.6$, $SD = 1.2$) followed by no-victim jokes ($M = 3.4$, $SD = 1.0$), then by female-victimizing jokes ($M = 2.7$, $SD = 1.2$). Men rated male-victimizing jokes ($M = 3.2$, $SD = 0.7$) and no-victim jokes ($M = 3.2$, $SD = 0.9$) comparably, and female-victimizing jokes funniest ($M = 3.9$, $SD = 1.2$), $F(2, 160) = 26.66$, $p < .001$, $p_{rep} > .986$. (Data from Beins et al., 2005)

This presentation is factually accurate, but who would want to wade through the string of numbers? Besides, it is difficult to make comparisons across groups based on this presentation. If these were your data, you could create either a table or a figure to depict them. Figure 6.1 provides the structure for a table that would represent the data more coherently.

In many published articles, the means appear next to the standard deviations, with the latter in parentheses, as illustrated in Figure 6.1. If, for some reason, you wanted to discuss differences between means separately from differences in standard deviations, you could present them in different places in the table, as shown in Figure 6.2.

Figures 6.1 and 6.2 both demonstrate how you can depict numbers showing differences among means. Researchers use other types of data, however, so you may need tables with somewhat different formats. For instance, if you

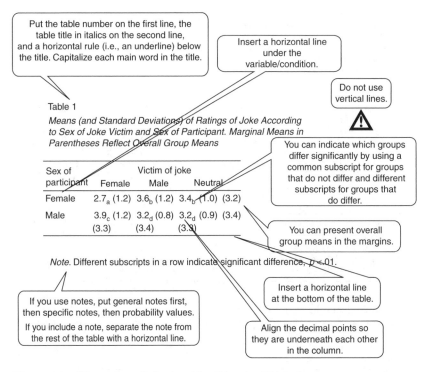

Figure 6.1 Illustration of a basic table of data in APA style.

want to present correlational data, the layout of your table will not be quite the same as when you present averages. If you measured several different variables and computed the correlations among them, a table like Figure 6.3 would illustrate the relations among the variables clearly. You can also create a table with only one column, but with rows as shown in Figure 6.3. You would then use the space bar to create the spacing you desire.

As you can see in Figures 6.1 and 6.3, you can put notes at the bottom of a table if it helps the reader understand the contents of the table. You insert a horizontal line and put any notes below the line. You may insert more than one note. General notes with a wide scope come first, followed by more specific notes (e.g., referring to individual groups), then probability notes related to significance levels.

When you create your table, you can simply type it, using the space bar to creating the spacing you want. Or you can use your word processor to create the table; this approach is often the most efficient and easiest. Table 6.5 shows how you can use Word© to format the table. Table 6.6 shows the final result.

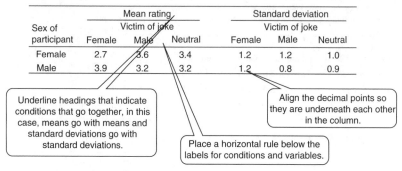

Figure 6.2 Example of a table in which different measurements (means and standard deviations) appear separately. This format is fairly rare in published articles.

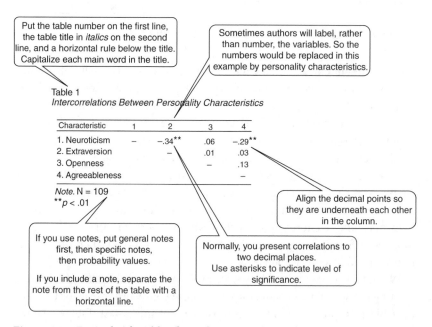

Figure 6.3 Example of a table of correlations in APA style.

Table 6.5 Creating a Table with Word[®]

Step 1	Type the table number on the first line, then type the table title in italics on the second line.
Step 2	Make a 5 × 5 table by selecting *Insert* in the toolbar at the top of the Word page. (For different tables, you might not use a 5 × 5 table. It depends on your research design.)
Step 3	Leave the upper left cell empty. In the first column, second row, indicate the first variable name (Sex of participant) and, below the variable name, the conditions for that variable (female and male), each in its own row. This is often the variable with fewer conditions.
Step 4	On the top line, first column, type the second variable name (Joke victim).
Step 5	• Highlight the top row of cells. • Right-click on the mouse and select *Merge cells*. • Center the variable name.
Step 6	On the second line, type the conditions of the second variable name, one per column. (In this case, Female, Male, Neutral.) This is often the variable with more conditions.

Now that you have established the structure of the table, enter the data.

Step 7	To erase all lines in the table: • Right-click on the mouse and select *Borders and Shading*. • Choose *None*. The lines in the table will disappear.
Step 8	To insert a line under the title of the table: • Highlight cells in the top row of the table. • Right-click on the mouse and choose *Borders and Shading*. • Click on the icon on the right that shows a line at the top of the cell. • Click on *OK*.
Step 9	To insert a line under the row listing the variables (Sex of participant: female, male, neutral): • Highlight the row listing the variables. • Right-click on the mouse and choose *Borders and Shading*. • Click on the icon on the right that shows a line at the bottom of the cell. • Click on *OK*.
Step 10	To insert a line at the bottom of the data: • Highlight cells in the bottom row of the table • Right-click on the mouse and choose *Borders and Shading*. • Click on the icon on the right that shows a line at the bottom of the cell. • Click on *OK*.
Step 11	To enter any notes below the bottom line: • Position the cursor below the table and type the notes.

Note: To create subscripts as you see in the completed table, click on the small arrow in the *Font* tab on the top of the Word page, then select subscript. When you finish typing the subscript, click on the *Font* arrow again and remove the check mark from the subscript box.

Table 6.6   The Result: Means (and Standard Deviations) of Ratings of Jokes According to Sex of Joke Victim and Sex of Participant. Marginal Means in Parentheses Reflect Overall Group Means

	Joke victim			
Sex of participant	*Female*	*Male*	*Neutral*	
Female	2.7$_a$ (1.2)	3.6$_b$ (1.2)	3.4$_b$ (1.0)	3.2
Male	3.9$_c$ (1.2)	3.2$_d$ (0.7)	3.2$_d$ (0.9)	3.4
	3.3	3.4	3.3	

Note: Different subscripts in a row indicate significant differences, *ps* < .01.

Creating Figures

Tables summarize large numbers of data efficiently and precisely. Sometimes, though, visual presentations using figures can be helpful. In a graph, it is not always possible to discern the exact values of the data, so using figures may entail sacrificing some precision. Figure 6.4 shows the standard elements of a graph that depicts comparisons among multiple groups.

Figure 6.5 illustrates the results of a study in which participants' moods were manipulated prior to their rating a set of jokes (data from Cronin, Fazio, & Beins, 1998). It would be possible (but not desirable because of the density of the information) to present the results in text as follows:

> Participants showed greater mirth in the elevated mood condition; that is, they exhibited more laughing, smiling, and outward signs of humor. In contrast, the participants showed nearly equal levels of mirth in the depressed and in the neutral conditions. For women in the depressed mood condition, $M = 0.64$ ($SD = 0.86$); for men in the depressed mood condition, $M = 0.86$ ($SD = 1.08$). For women in the elevated and neutral conditions, $M = 0.66$ ($SD = 0.65$) and $M = 0.67$ ($SD = 0.68$), respectively. For men in the elevated and neutral conditions, $M = 1.70$ ($SD = 1.64$) and $M = 1.22$ ($SD = 1.35$), respectively.

I hope that it has become clear to you that simply listing a series of numbers can be an accurate way to present data but not a particularly effective way to generate understanding on the part of the reader. It is just too hard to keep all the numbers in mind to see how they relate to one another.

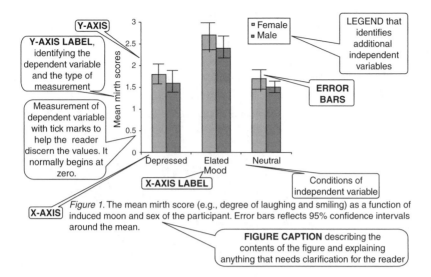

Figure 1. The mean mirth score (e.g., degree of laughing and smiling) as a function of induced moon and sex of the participant. Error bars reflects 95% confidence intervals around the mean.

Figure 6.4 Graph with labels of common elements of the graph. This is a bar graph, but the same general principles hold for any graph, such as line graphs, showing comparisons across groups. Line graphs are appropriate when the variable on the X-axis is quantitative. In your manuscript, the figure caption appears below the figure. The figure caption should include any explanatory information needed to understand the graph. In preparing a manuscript, you would place the caption and the figure on their own separate page, one caption and figure to a page.

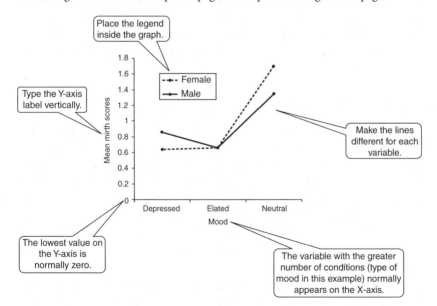

Figure 6.5 A line graph showing the extent of mirth expressions like laughing and smiling as a function of mood of research participants. Note that the Y-axis starts with the value of zero.

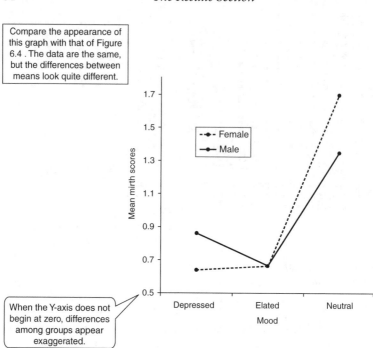

Figure 6.6 Line graph in APA style. Normally, the Y-axis begins with zero. When it does not, the results may be deceptive. In this graph, the data are the same as those in Figure 6.5, but the differences across conditions on the X-axis seem greater because of the change of the scale of the Y-axis. Figures do not generally use notes the way tables do.

If you refer to Figures 6.5 and 6.6, you will see that the pattern of data looks somewhat different, even though both of these figures depict the same information. One of the important considerations in creating graphs is that you can alter their appearance greatly by changing the scale of the X- and Y-axes. The data don't change, but their appearance does. The data in Figure 6.5 are based on the same data as Figure 6.6, but the scale on the Y-axis has changed. In Figure 6.5, the Y-axis begins with a value of zero whereas Figure 6.6 begins 0.5, and it is lengthened vertically. These changes in the structure of the graph lead to a very noticeable change in appearance.

If your Y-axis begins at a number greater than zero, small differences can be magnified. Further, if you extend the Y-axis so that it is quite long compared with the X-axis, the differences between groups will look big; if you compress the Y-axis so that it is quite short compared with the X-axis, the differences between groups will look small.

The appearance of the graph should match the accurate message you want to convey. You need to make sure that you are not deceiving your reader by portraying the data so that they lead to an inaccurate conclusion.

The figures described so far have related to comparison of separate groups, which lends itself to bar and line graphs. If your research involves correlational data, however, your data will probably lend themselves to scatter diagrams. The principles involved in creating a scatter diagram are similar to those for bar charts and line graphs. An example of a scatter diagram appears in Figure 6.7.

One final type of figure to be discussed here is the frequency histogram. It looks like a bar graph, but its main function is to illustrate how many observations fall into different categories. In the histogram shown in Figure 6.8, you can see how many students thought they had unhealthy lifestyles (low ratings) versus healthy lifestyles (high ratings) based on the results of

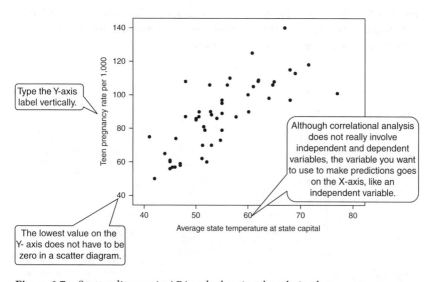

Figure 6.7 Scatter diagram in APA style showing the relation between temperature and teen birth rates in the states in the US and example of a figure caption. A scatter diagram is appropriate for showing the pattern of individual cases measured on two different variables. In this example, there is a significant positive correlation, reflecting the fact that as the temperature increases, so does the teen pregnancy rate. Because this relation is correlational, however, you cannot draw any conclusions about cause and effect.

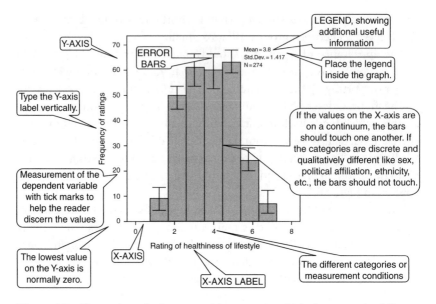

Figure 6.8 Illustration of a frequency histogram in which the categories fall on a continuum. In this case, the categories are ratings that progress from 1 to 7. In such a histogram, the bars should touch one another.

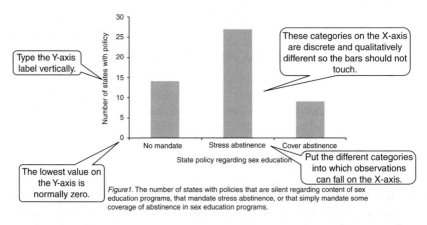

Figure1. The number of states with policies that are silent regarding content of sex education programs, that mandate stress abstinence, or that simply mandate some coverage of abstinence in sex education programs.

Figure 6.9 Illustration of a frequency histogram with discrete (nonquantitative) categories on the X-axis. When the categories are discrete, the bars should not touch.

student responses to a question about their lifestyles. When the X-axis involves a quantitative variable, the bars should touch.

In Figure 6.9, you see how to format the graph when the X-axis involves a qualitative, categorical variable. In this case, the bars do not touch.

The Connection Between the Text and the Tables and Figures

The advantage of creating tables and figures in your manuscript is that you can present a large amount of data in a small amount of space. You should use them judiciously, though, because tables and figures require a relatively large amount of space, and journals are limited in the number of pages they are allowed to print. Your instructor may want you to create tables and figures for practice, but in writing professionally, you need to decide if they are worth the space they require.

That is, could you get your point across as easily and effectively by using words rather than pictures? If the answer is yes, you probably do not need tables or figures. On the other hand, if your reader's work will be easier because of a table or a figure, you should include it.

When you include visual elements in your manuscript, refer to them in your text. Don't just create them and expect the reader to pay attention to them. You must connect the figure or table to the text so the reader knows the relation between the two. Furthermore, if the text gets the point across, you don't need a table or figure. If you can express a result more efficiently in a table or figure, don't include that information in the text. In the end, the text and the tables and figures should complement, not duplicate, one another.

The Difference Between Results and Discussion Sections

In most APA-style papers, you create separate sections for describing your data and saying whether those data support your hypotheses (Results) and for talking about what your results mean (Discussion). As such, in your Results section, you should present your data without interpreting what they mean. This does not mean that you give only a cursory presentation of your data; rather, it means that you consider only the data and the statistical results. You offer descriptive statistics such as means and standard deviations, accompanied by inferential statistics such as the ANOVA. At this point, you don't link your results to theory or other related research.

Your Results section should be fairly noncontroversial because you are giving your reader numerical facts and, for the most part, the facts are straightforward. Sometimes, results spark controversy, such as when researchers criticize the statistical approach used by earlier authors. But this type of disagreement is relatively rare because psychologists have generally agreed on many statistical approaches. In essence, there should be no controversy because every statement you make in your Results section should describe and be linked directly to your data.

As an example, if you look at Figure 6.5, you will see that participants showed more mirth responses in an elevated-mood condition than in either depressed- or neutral-mood conditions. This is a straightforward result that nobody could deny—the data reflect that pattern of behavior. So it would be appropriate to include this in the results. On the other hand, you would refrain from interpreting the data and saying what is going on in the participants' heads. Your conclusion may have validity, but it is an interpretation. It is not a fact in the same sense as noting that means for the different mood groups differ. Inferences and conclusions belong in the Discussion section, which contains speculation, interpretation, theory, and connection to other research.

Some Final Points About Presenting Results

As you have undoubtedly noticed, there are some fairly specific guidelines for presenting the results of research. If you refer to the *Publication Manual of the American Psychological Association* (American Psychological Association, 2010), you will see that it devotes eight pages to presentation of numbers and statistics. Sometimes the rules seem picky and maybe even nonsensical. But psychologists follow these rules in writing.

Some final points about presenting numerical information appear in Table 6.7. This is an encapsulation of the entire set of APA guidelines about presentation of statistics and data. For presentation involving rare occurrences, you can consult the APA *Publication Manual*. You can also peruse published journal articles to see how researchers have presented this type of information.

Table 6.7 Specific Rules and Guidelines Commonly Used for Presenting Numbers and Statistics in APA Style

Rule	Examples
Write out numbers less than ten. Use a numeral for numbers equal to 10 or more. Exception: If you are giving a series of numbers that includes values greater than 10, use all numerals.	• Participants learned six lists. • There were 15 participants. • Participants learned 6, 8, or 10 lists.
Do not start sentences with numerals. Preferably, start the sentence non-numerically. If you need to start a sentence with a number, write out the number.	• Volunteers included 40 students recruited from psychology classes. • Forty students from psychology classes participated.
Use numbers to represent time and dates, number of participants, scores on a scale.	• 1 hr 22 min • February 27, 1980 • 8 participants (but eight people) • The Likert-type scale ranged from 1 (*low*) to 7 (*high*).
Use numerals for precise measurements. Abbreviate the units of measurement, but do not use periods after the abbreviation except to avoid confusion.	• 10 min (for 10 minutes) • 25 cm (for 25 centimeters) • 10 in. (for 10 inches) (Use a period here so the reader does not think that you are using the preposition in.)
Put spaces between elements in mathematical copy. For an inferential statistic, do not put a space between the statistic and the number of degrees of freedom.	• $t(35) = 1.02, p > .05$ *not* $t(35)=1.02, p>.05$

(Continued)

Table 6.7 (cont'd)

Rule	Examples
If a measurement could be greater than one but is actually less than one, use a zero before the decimal point.	• 0.35 (if the value could have been greater than one, such as in measuring length) • .35 (if the value could not be greater than one, such as a probability value or a correlation coefficient)
Carry inferential statistics to two decimal places. Use two more decimal places than were used in the raw data.	• $F(2, 114) = 1.71, p = .185$ • If the raw data are whole numbers (e.g., 1, 3, 4), report summary statistics like means to two decimal places: $M = 3.67$.
Use an uppercase N for total sample size and lowercase n to represent subsamples. You can use a subscript to identify particular subsamples.	• $N = 100$ (for a total of 100 participants) • $n = 25$ (for a subsample) • $n_{girls} = 25$ (for the number of girls in a group)
Use the symbol for percent (%) when it is used with a numeral; use the word percentage if there is no number. If the percentage starts a sentence, write out the words (e.g., Sixty percent). If the percentage appears mid-sentence, use numerals and the percent sign (e.g., 60%). Exception: Always use the symbol in tables to save space.	• 10% • A different percentage of respondents.
When symbols are in Roman letters (e.g., N, p), italicize them. When symbols are Greek, do not italicize them.	• $N = 25$ (N is italicized) • $\mu = 25$ (mu is not italicized)

7

The Discussion Section

Nothing is so simple that it cannot be misunderstood.

Freeman Teague, Jr.

That is what learning is. You suddenly understood something you've understood all your life, but in a new way.

Doris Lessing

Imagine that you knew something about behavior that nobody else in the world knew. You could do one of two things with the knowledge. You could keep it to yourself or you could shout it from the rooftops.

What do researchers do in this situation? After doing a project, only fairly bizarre psychologists shout their findings from actual rooftops. Instead, they write papers for journals, which is actually a psychologist's way of shouting from the rooftops. After you carry out a study, it is nice to let others know what you have found and what it means. That is what the Discussion section is for.

In this chapter, you will see how you can tie together all the information in the previous sections of your research paper. The Discussion section revisits the basic concepts of interest to you and how you addressed your research questions; this section also shows how your results supported your ideas. Finally, the Discussion allows you to speculate on what you think your data are telling you.

If you think back to the chapter on the Introduction section, you may recall that there were some general questions that were relevant to your opening ideas: What are you doing? What do psychologists already know about the topic? Why is it interesting? How will it advance our knowledge? What do

APA Style Simplified: Writing in Psychology, Education, Nursing, and Sociology,
First Edition. Bernard C. Beins.

you expect to happen and why? In the Discussion, you explain the ideas you were considering and what you did with them, tell the reader how your results relate to what other psychologists have found and why your ideas should be of interest to psychologists, and whether your expectations were supported.

In general, in the Method and Results sections of your paper, you limit your presentation to your research project. In the Discussion section, however, you are beginning a conversation with the reader about your ideas. What does your study have to say about the topics of interest to you, and where do your ideas lead? Your job here is to stimulate your reader to think about larger issues. You have to develop clear explanations that make sense to the reader and that show why your work is interesting and important.

Summarizing Your Results

You should refresh your reader at the beginning of the Discussion about what you discovered. You will be doing your reader a favor if you present each of your research findings separately, perhaps reserving a paragraph or two for each finding or closely related group of findings. Begin with your most interesting and important results.

The reiteration of the results should not include statistics. Rather, give a verbal description that encapsulates the critical findings. If the reader is interested in the statistics, they are available in the Results section; there is no need to repeat them here. In addition, you don't want to spend too much time repeating what you just said in the Results section; a brief summary will suffice.

You can see in Box 7.1 how Enguidanos, Kogan, Keefe, Geron, and Katz (2011) repeated the gist of their results to begin the discussion of what those results mean for the practice of social work with elderly patients. They identified key points of the results without any statistics. This approach reinstates in the reader's mind the questions important in the research.

Kaiser, Vick, and Major (2006) took a somewhat different approach. They studied whether people pay attention to different environmental cues when they expect to experience prejudice. In the Discussion section of their research article, they began their discussion by noting that they hypothesized that individuals who chronically anticipate being a target of prejudice, or who find themselves in a situation in which these concerns are salient, are vigilant for cues that their social identity is under threat. Box 7.1 shows you how they initiated their conclusions.

When you describe your results, connect them to your hypotheses, which you should have developed in the Introduction. That is, state whether your results provided support for your hypotheses. As Kaiser et al. (2006) showed, a simple statement often suffices.

If you have developed multiple hypotheses, deal with each one individually. There is nothing wrong with reporting that the results did not match your expectations. As we all know, human behavior is complex and not easy to predict. So your data might confirm a hypothesis entirely, partially, or not at all. Research is a process of finding out the limits to our theories and our predictions.

Box 7.1   Examples of Approaches to Starting the Discussion Section

Brief Restatement of the Results

This article examined problems identified by older adult primary care patients with multiple chronic conditions and their social worker and physician. Although problems represented a diverse list of concerns, issues surrounding health and management of health conditions were most often identified by patients. Although exercise and weight loss problems were most prevalent, issues surrounding meals and financial/legal concerns were more likely to be resolved during the course of the study. This may be due to the ease in solving these types of problems; although some health improvement goals may be long-term (e.g., weight loss), arranging for meal delivery services or attending congregate meals can be solved easily through enrollment in such programs. (Enguidanos, Kogan, Keefe, Geron, & Katz, 2011, pp. 286–287)

Statement About the Research Hypotheses

Our research findings were consistent with this hypothesis. We found that individuals with chronic or situationally induced concerns about prejudice preconsciously screen their environment for signs of identity devaluation. (Kaiser et al., 2006. p. 337)

Restatement of the General Purpose of the Research

In the present study, we considered four models that account for the relation between WM [working memory] and later problem solving performance in elementary school children. Before discussing the findings related to these models, two questions that directed this study are addressed. (Swanson, 2011, p. 11)

Connecting Different Aspects of Your Results

If you have included multiple dependent variables (DVs) in your study or if your research report involves more than one study, you should tell how the separate components relate to one another. For example, if you had more than one DV, say how the different DVs combine to give a more complete picture of your participants' behaviors and responses. That is, what do two (or more) DVs tell you that one alone would not?

Sometimes your different measurements will complement one another. When this happens, you can make a stronger argument about your conclusions than if you had a single DV. On the other hand, sometimes different DVs lead to different results because those measurements tap into different aspects of behavior. In your discussion of your results, you should bring together these individual results so you can develop a complete picture of participants' behaviors.

For example, my students and I conducted several projects in which participants read and responded to a series of jokes after their moods were temporarily raised or depressed. One DV was the participant's rating of how funny the joke was; the second DV was the degree of mirth (e.g., laughing, smiling) that the participant showed.

In initial experiments, our only dependent measure had been joke ratings (Cronin et al., 1998). The participant's mood (elevated vs. depressed) had no effect on the ratings of the jokes. People in depressed moods rated the jokes just as the people in the elevated group did. But when we added mirth responses as a second DV, we found that mood did have an effect on responses to jokes. People in the elevated mood group showed greater degrees of mirth than the people in the depressed group did; that is, they laughed and smiled more (Martin & McGaffick, 2001).

It appears that mood does not affect the rated funniness of jokes, but mood does affect the overt reactions to the jokes. If we had used only one DV (joke ratings), we would not have seen that mood has a reliable effect on the way people respond to jokes.

Sometimes if you use multiple DVs, they don't cooperate, providing contradictory results. Although, as a researcher, you don't really want to encounter this situation, it is important to recognize when it occurs. You can't simply ignore it. If you can figure out a reason for such inconsistency, you should report it. On the other hand, sometimes you can't figure out why the results occurred the way they did. In that case, simply say so.

Dealing With Nonsignificant Results

Sometimes your data analysis will lead to results that are statistically nonsignificant. (Remember that psychologists refer to results that don't achieve statistical significance as *nonsignificant*, not as *insignificant*.) Such results are problematic because you won't know whether the results are nonsignificant because there is no relation between the variables that you are investigating, because of random error, or because there was a problem with the design of your study.

Another possible explanation for a nonsignificant effect could be low power due to too small a sample size and a small effect size. However, in many cases, sample size is not a very sound argument; there are often more critical reasons for failure to attain significance. If you raise it as an issue, you should make a strong logical case about why the sample size is important. Issues of sample size can be relevant if the data are quite variable or if an effect is real but weak, but as long as your sample size is more or less consistent with other, similar research, an argument based on sample size is not going to be very convincing. The problem, unfortunately, is that when nonsignificant effects occur, it can be very difficult to figure out why.

You might have hypothesized that you would see nonsignificant results because that is what other researchers had discovered or because a theory predicts no relation among variables. If your nonsignificant results were as you expected, that can provide support for your ideas. On the other hand, if you expected significance but didn't see it, it may not be clear what you can say about it in your Discussion. You might not be able to say much more than that you are puzzled by the results and have no explanation.

Sometimes, your results will be significant, but totally puzzling. As you will recall from your knowledge of statistics, researchers usually set a Type I error rate of 5% in their research. So if you conduct enough analyses, some results (i.e., about 5%) will be statistically significant, even though the difference between groups or the correlation between variables does not mean anything and would probably not replicate if you repeated the study. If you wind up with significant effects that are completely unexpected and totally puzzling, simply state that there is no convincing explanation for the results except that it might be a Type I error. In such a situation, it does not make sense to try and conjure up complex and convoluted explanations. It is reasonable, though, to suggest another study that would determine if the results were reliable.

Comparing Your Results With Those of Others

After you have drawn the connection between your results and your hypotheses, you can take the opportunity to link your research to previous studies. Furthermore, your ideas will have greater credibility if you can connect them to the work of other investigators. If you haven't found research that relates to yours, you have probably not searched extensively enough.

Sometimes your results will be consistent with previous research, but sometimes there will be discrepancies. Investigators report this kind of outcome in published research rather often. For instance, in Box 7.2, you can see how different authors have dealt with results that support previous research and results that contradict previous studies. As an example of how researchers have made such connections, consider the work of Reder et al. (2006) They studied drug-induced amnesia, using the drug midazolam, which blocks memory formation in people; in their Discussion, they explicitly linked their data to several previous studies with which their findings were consistent.

On the other hand, Cheung and Ngai (2007) investigated social work outreach and discovered results that conflicted with earlier research. In such a case, authors typically try to address the issue of why the discrepancies occurred as they did.

Just as your results may or may not conform to your hypotheses, they may or may not be similar to those of previous researchers. There are different reasons for such an outcome. The other research might have had methodological limitations or yours might have. Different types of participants in the studies or different species of subjects might have led to different outcomes.

Still, it is important to try and determine why your replication did not achieve the same results. Wang (2006) investigated people's first memories from their childhoods and generally obtained results very similar to expectations and to previous research. However, there was one element of the findings that differed from earlier work: Wang's research involved a slightly different memory task, which may have accounted for the difference, as they noted.

> The ages of earliest memories were substantially later in the current study than in previous studies using free-recall tasks ... or asking participants to answer questions about targeted events such as the birth of a sibling. ... The differences between the current study and previous studies ... are particularly interesting. ... This issue merits further investigation, and examination of

both the accessibility and the content of early memories elicited in different experimental paradigms will be necessary to unravel the mystery of infantile amnesia. (Wang, 2006, p. 713).

Box 7.2   Examples of Connections Between Current and Previous Research

Statements Showing Support for Previous Research Results

Our data are consistent with the results of Huppert and Piercy (1976, 1978), who found that patients with anterograde amnesia can still recognize pictures as long as judgments do not require list discrimination .... Our results are also consistent with the priming study of Musen et al. (1999), which showed that it is easier to create an association to a word than to an unfamiliar stimulus. Our hypothesis that familiarity affects the probability of encoding as well as the probability of a false alarm can also explain a finding of Koutstaal et al. (Reder et al., 2006, p. 565)

Statements Failing to Show Support for Previous Research

Results show that the at-risk youths display lower delinquency when they participate more frequently in developmental group activities organized by outreaching social workers, spend less time with friends, or spend more time with their family.... These findings are consistent with Hypotheses 1 and 2, which rest on the principle of need matching. ...

The finding that developmental group activities are more beneficial for reducing the delinquency of youths who spend less time with family is contradictory to the expectation that family support is necessary to bolster the benefit of social services (Okwunnabua & Durea, 1998). (Cheung & Ngai, 2007, p. 160)

Stating the Importance and Implications of Your Results

After you conduct your study, you will know something that, literally, nobody else in the world knows. You have created knowledge that did not exist before you completed your project. This can be an exciting thought because, as Francis Bacon wrote, "*Nam et ipsa, scientia potestas est,*" which means "In and of itself, knowledge is power."

You will probably see the importance of your results more clearly than anybody else will, so you are in the best position to illustrate to the reader how your study has advanced knowledge about people. The Discussion section is the most appropriate place to write about the importance of your ideas. For example, if a theory makes a prediction, your data could lend support to the power of that theory. Or, if your data are inconsistent with the theory, you can help establish the limitations of the theory or, perhaps, to extend it in new directions.

One important task for your Discussion is to convince your reader that your question is meaningful. That is, tell why professionals would think that your research has contributed to our knowledge base. You can't accomplish this merely by saying that your question is important. You need to connect your research with current thought and theory. That is, how does your research relate to what others have been studying?

The Discussion section also lets you expand your presentation beyond the confines of your particular research project. Every study leaves questions unanswered, and no single study answers all of the interesting questions in an area. So in your Discussion, you can tell the reader how your research has paved the way for new ideas by answering some questions and giving suggestion for others. The research by Wang (2006) on infantile memory cited above provides a good illustration of this. Scientists are impressed not only by clever and insightful research projects, but also by the implications that those projects have for future research.

So, for instance, if you conducted your study in a laboratory, you could take the opportunity to speculate on how your findings might relate to every-day life. Likewise, you could relate your results to a different population of participants or to different stimuli and materials. This kind of conjecture shows that you are conversant with the important issues in the area.

Acknowledging the Limitations of Your Study

No study is perfect. That fact is a reality of life. In your Discussion, you should acknowledge the limitations of your study. These limitations can involve different facets of your project.

For example, your methodology might set the limits to generalizability of your data. When planning your study, you have to make decisions about what kinds of measurements to make or what conditions to study. If you make different measurements or create different types of groups, your results might turn out differently. In dealing with this kind of limitation, you should not assume that you made poor choices for your measurements and conditions. Rather, you should simply recognize that there is more work to be done to answer your question fully. Furthermore, when it comes to questions of measurements and conditions, it isn't necessary to belabor the limitations. If you are carrying out your research with measurements that are identical to those of previous researchers, other investigators are probably not likely to question your study because of those measurements.

Another limitation to your study may involve your sample. If your participants were students, your results might generalize well to other students, but maybe not to nonstudents or to people of different ages. Or, if your participants included mostly females, your results might not generalize well to males. As always, you should use good judgment and your knowledge of the phenomena you are studying to draw your conclusions. Some phenomena may exhibit themselves similarly for women and for men, so if your study included mostly women, your conclusions might generalize nicely to men. Still, you should make sure that you acknowledge such limitations if they are potentially relevant.

Another potential limitation involves identifying causal relations. If your study was correlational or quasi-experimental, you should avoid suggesting that you can identify the cause of your participants' responses. This caution is particularly important when your study involves a quasi-experimental design that involves intact groups and when participants are not randomly assigned to conditions. A quasi-experimental design looks like an experimental design that permits causal conclusions, but, in reality, quasi-experiments are correlational designs that have as their purpose the comparison of groups, just as experiments do.

8

References
Citations in the Text and the Reference List

Don't worry about people stealing an idea. If it's original, you will have to ram it down their throats.

Howard Aiken

All of us ... need to take advice and to receive help from other people.

Alexis Carrell

If no other investigator had a research idea like yours, you would be the most unusual person in the world. Good research virtually never arises spontaneously and without any earlier work on the topic. So if you come up with an idea, it makes sense to see who else has had a similar idea. This is where references are important.

In this chapter, you will see how to present the citations for previous work to which you have referred. The References section may very well be the least glamorous part of a research report and the most mechanical, but it is still very important. Each person builds on the ideas of others. When you cite previous work, you are documenting the flow of ideas from one thinker to another. The references you use tell your reader what path you took to arrive at your research question and your conclusions. This chapter deals with the way you refer to citations in your writing and how you list them in the References section.

Choosing the references to use can sometimes be difficult. You may have a great number of potential sources to cite, but you may not want to mention them all because there will be too much redundancy. So you should

APA Style Simplified: Writing in Psychology, Education, Nursing, and Sociology, First Edition. Bernard C. Beins.
© 2012 John Wiley & Sons, Inc. Published 2012 by John Wiley & Sons, Inc.

identify the points you want to make and decide which of your references will help you develop your ideas. Sometimes writers have a tendency to want to mention every single source they encounter. If you do this, you run the risk of overwhelming your reader.

The References section in an APA-style paper has a particular purpose: It lists the work you have referred to in your writing. So if you mention a book, a book chapter, a journal article, or any other source, you should include that source in your References section. If you do not mention a source in your paper, do not include it among the references. In other disciplines, a paper might have a Bibliography that contains work not cited in the paper, but in APA style, we only include in the References the sources we actually mention in the paper.

There are too many details regarding reference citation to list exhaustively here. However, examples of the major types of citations appear at the end of this chapter. If you need to cite a source that is not included here, you should refer to the *Publication Manual of the American Psychological Association* (American Psychological Association, 2010).

Finally, you should keep in mind that the references begin on a separate page in a paper you write. Other sections of the paper simply start on the line after the final sentence of the preceding section. For example, the heading for the Results section begins right after the final sentence of the Method section, without any extra lines between sections. The References section is different in that it starts on its own page. Like the rest of your paper, it is double spaced. So type the section heading (i.e., the word References, centered in bold type) followed on the next line by the first reference. Do not include a blank line after each reference.

Citing References in the Text

There are several ways of citing references as your create your text, but all of them involve mentioning the author or authors and the year in which the source was published or presented. You use last names only unless there are different authors with the same last name, which could confuse a reader; in that case, use the initials of the different authors in addition to the last name. Furthermore, it is almost never useful to cite an author's affiliation (e.g., Ithaca College) because it generally does not matter where a writer works. So the referencing style within the body of your paper is simple: last names of the author(s) and year of the work.

If you want to present an overall sense of the ideas of several writers, you can present your idea, then refer to those writers as a group. When you do this, you alphabetize the references in the parentheses by the last name of the first author, then separate different authors' works with a semicolon. You can see an example of this below.

When you alphabetize names, you alphabetize by the last name of the first author. You never rearrange names of the authors of an individual reference. The order of names in your References section needs to match the order of names in the published article.

As a rule, each time you cite somebody's work, you include the names and the year of publication or presentation of the ideas. However, if you have just mentioned a source, you may not need to cite the year again. The general rule is that, within a given paragraph, you need to include the year only once. In subsequent paragraphs it is often a good idea to repeat the year so the reader is certain which source you are citing. If you are providing a long discussion of a single reference, you may not need to include the year in each paragraph because there is little chance that the reader will be confused as to which work you are citing.

Citing One or Two Authors

Scientific publications very often include more than one author. When there are one or two authors, the format is entirely straightforward. Every time you mention work with one or two authors, you cite all names and the date.

As an example, consider Scheibe's (2004) discussion of media literacy in which she cited two previous works as follows:

> Even with a growing emphasis on technology skills and critical thinking, there are still only seven states that mandate media literacy as a separate strand in their state standards (**Baker, 2004**), and even those states have had difficulty grappling with how to assess media literacy as part of standardized state testing.
>
> **Kubcy and Baker (2000)** have noted, however, that nearly all states do refer to aspects of media literacy education as part of the mandated state standards, although they do not typically use the phrase *media literacy*. (Scheibe, 2004, p. 62)

One of the citations inserts the author within parentheses. The second citation mentions the authors in the text and puts the year of their work within parentheses. The citations are in bold in the example above just to show you how they look. Do not put them in bold in your own work.

Citing Sources With Three to Five Authors

If a publication or presentation involved three to five authors, you identify all the authors when you first mention the work. Then, in subsequent references to them, you list only the first author and follow it with this phrase "et al." (There should be a period after the phrase.) For instance, Stephenson, Pena-Shaff, and Quirk (2006) identified predictors of suicidal ideation among college students, citing the work of previous researchers:

> Suicide rates for college students are about 7.5 per 100,000 per year but older students and males are at greater risk (Silverman, Meyer, Sloan, Raffel, & Pratt, 1997)....
>
> In general, while the suicide rates of college student populations are lower than those of their non-college peers, many of the predictors of suicide are the same (Silverman et al., 1997). (Stephenson et al., 2006, p. 109)

As you can see in this quotation, the first citation includes all the authors of the work by Silverman and his colleagues. The second citation mentions only the first author followed by "et al." There is a period after *al.*

Citing Sources With Six or More Authors

Occasionally, a large group of people collaborate to create a publication or presentation. If there are six or more such people, the referencing format is a little different than when there are five or fewer. The referencing style below is appropriate for the work cited because there are 18 authors of the journal article. It would take up a lot of space and not be particularly useful to list all of them.

> Academic psychologists are teachers as well as scholars. However, only recently have people noted the feasibility and the importance of linking the two (e.g., Halpern et al., 1998; ...). (Beins, 2006, p. 11)

In this citation, Halpern is the only name that appears in the text. The first time you mention a reference in the body of your manuscript, cite all authors if there are five or fewer. In APA style, if there are six or more authors, you list only the first author, followed by et al. (with a period after *al*), which means *and others* in Latin, and the date of publication.

When a source involves more than seven authors, you type it in the References section a little differently than you would a source with fewer than seven. You include the names of only the first six authors, then you put a comma after the sixth author's initials and then type three ellipsis points (...) followed by the name of the final author. This format omits the names of some authors altogether.

Citing Personal Communications

Sometimes you will have had communication with a scholar who has provided useful information that has not appeared in print. When this happens, you should refer to the communication in the text, but you do not list it in the References section.

Beins (2006) cited such personal communication, which includes the name of the person, an indication that it was a personal communication, and the date on which the communication occurred:

> Teachers of psychology who submit materials to OTRP need to remember that the focus of materials published in OTRP is utilitarian. Theoretical justification for the project and the background literature are less important for resources in OTRP (Janet Carlson, personal communication, August 10, 2004). (Beins, 2006, p. 13)

Including this type of information gives appropriate credit to the person whose idea you mention, and it establishes the date, which could be important if the person changes his or her thoughts about the topic at some point.

Citing Multiple Sources Within Parentheses

If you cite more than one work within parentheses, there are certain rules for ordering them.

- Alphabetize the references by the last name of the first author.
- If you cite the same author more than once, put the author's work in chronological order, with the oldest first.
- If you cite an author who has more than one reference in a given year, add letters to the date (e.g., Davis, 2004a, 2004b, 2004c).

- Separate references to a single author or group of authors with a comma (e.g., Davis, 2002, 2004, 2006).
- Separate different authors or groups of authors with a semicolon (Davis, 2002, 2004, 2006; Smith, 1995).

Order of Citations in the Reference List

- The most basic rule is to alphabetize the reference list by the last name of the first author.
- If you cite two references for which the first author is the same for each, put them in chronological order.
- If you cite two references with the same first author, but different coauthors, alphabetize by the last name of the second (or third, etc.) author.
- If two references have the same authors, but one of the references has an additional author cited at the end, put the citation with fewer authors first in the reference list.
- Alphabetize names related to the Gaelic *Mac*, including *Mc*, *Mac*, and *M'* using the exact letters in the name. So *Mac* would come before *Mc*, which would come before *M'*. Similarly, a last name like *Saint James* would come before *St. James*.
- If two different authors have the same last name, alphabetize by their initials (e.g., Smith, R. A. would precede Smith, S. L.)
- If a group has authored a work, use the first important word of the group name as the author's name. (Words like *The* or *An* are not considered important words, so you would ignore them in alphabetizing the work.)

Using Your Word-Processing Program to Create the Citation

In APA style references, the first line of the citation falls on the left margin. Each succeeding line is indented five spaces. This format is called a *hanging indent*. You could type in your reference, hitting the *Enter* key at the end of each line. But if you change your margins or insert or remove a word, the spacing of the citation may be inappropriate. It is easier to use your word processor to format the reference.

Using Word® to create a hanging indent

Type the reference in proper format without worrying about the hanging indent.

Select *Format* on the menu at the top, then *Paragraph*, then *Indents and Spacing*.

In the area labeled *Indentation* select the dropdown box *Special*. Highlight and select *Hanging*.

Click on *OK*.

Examples of How Different Types of References Should Be Laid Out

- Alphabetize the references using last names and initials of authors. Keeps authors, names in the same order as in the original work.
- Using a hanging indent so that the first line is on the left margin and subsequent lines are indented.

When a single author is referenced multiple times, use chronological order; that is, put the oldest first.

When a single author is referenced multiple times, put the citations with the fewest coauthors first.

When there are more than seven authors, list the first six, followed by three ellipsis points, then the final author.

Beins, B. C. (1993). Writing assignments in statistics classes encourage students to learn interpretation. *Teaching of Psychology, 20,* 161–164. doi: 10.1207/s15328023top2003_6

Beins, B. C. (2006). The scholarship of teaching and pedagogy. In W. Buskist and S. F. Davis (Eds.), *Handbook of teaching of psychology* (pp. 11–15). Malden, MA: Blackwell.

Beins, B. C. Agnitti, J., Baldwin, V., Lapham, H., Yarmosky, S., Bubel, A., & MacNaughton, K., & Pashka, N. (2005, October). How expectations affect perception of offensive humor. Poster presented at the annual convention of the New England Psychological Association, New Haven, CT.

Halpern, D. F., Smothergill, D. W., Allen, M., Baker, S., Baum, C., Best, D. … Weaver, K. A. (1998). Scholarship in psychology: A paradigm for the twenty-first century. *American Psychologist, 53,* 1292–1297. doi: 10.1037/0003-066X.53.12.1292

Holmes, J. D. (2009). Transparency of self-report racial attitude scales. *Basic and Applied Social Psychology, 31,* 95–101. doi: 10.1080/01973530902876884

Mathie, V. A., Buskist, W., Carlson, J. F., David, S. F., Johnson, D. E., & Smith, R. A. (2004). Expanding the boundaries of scholarship in psychology through teaching, research, service, and administration. *Teaching of Psychology, 31,* 233–240. doi: 10.1207/s15328023top3104_2

Rader, N., & Vaughn, L. A. (2000). Infant reaching to a hidden affordance: Evidence for intentionality. *Infant Behavior & Development, 23,* 531–541. doi: 10.1016/S0163-6383(01)00060-1

Scheibe, C. L. (2004). A deeper sense of literacy: Curriculum-driven approaches to media literacy in the K-12 classroom. *The American Behavioral Scientist, 48,* 60–68. doi: 10.1177/0002764204267251

Stephenson, H., Pena-Shaff, J., & Quirk, P. (2006). Predictors of college student suicidal ideation: Gender differences. *College Student Journal, 40,* 109–117.

When there are seven or fewer authors, list them all.

Most journal articles have a doi designation. Include it if the article has one.

Not all journal articles have a doi designation.

Articles in Periodicals

Reference to a journal article

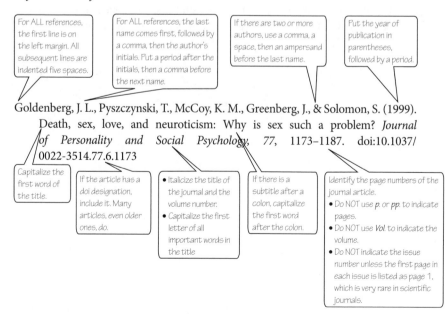

For ALL references, the first line is on the left margin. All subsequent lines are indented five spaces.

For ALL references, the last name comes first, followed by a comma, then the author's initials. Put a period after the initials, then a comma before the next name.

If there are two or more authors, use a comma, a space, then an ampersand before the last name.

Put the year of publication in parentheses, followed by a period.

Goldenberg, J. L., Pyszczynski, T., McCoy, K. M., Greenberg, J., & Solomon, S. (1999). Death, sex, love, and neuroticism: Why is sex such a problem? *Journal of Personality and Social Psychology, 77,* 1173–1187. doi:10.1037/0022-3514.77.6.1173

Capitalize the first word of the title.

If the article has a doi designation, include it. Many articles, even older ones, do.

- Italicize the title of the journal and the volume number.
- Capitalize the first letter of all important words in the title

If there is a subtitle after a colon, capitalize the first word after the colon.

Identify the page numbers of the journal article.
- Do NOT use *p.* or *pp.* to indicate pages.
- Do NOT use *Vol.* to indicate the volume.
- Do NOT indicate the issue number unless the first page in each issue is listed as page 1, which is very rare in scientific journals.

Reference to an article published online in advance of the printing of the journal

The format is almost identical to that of a journal article actually in print. It is good practice to update the citation in your paper when the print article appears.

Cite the actual date of online publication (NOT the date you retrieved it).

Swanson, H. L. (2011, August 22). Working memory, attention, and mathematical problem solving: A longitudinal study of elementary school children. *Journal of Educational Psychology*. Advance online publication. doi:10.1037/ a0025114

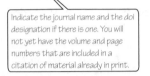

Indicate the journal name and the doi designation if there is one. You will not yet have the volume and page numbers that are included in a citation of material already in print.

Indicate that this is an advance online publication.

Reference to an Internet-only journal article

Indicate the exact date of publication in as much detail as possible.

Anderson, P. B., Spruille, B., Venable, R. H., & Strano, D. A. (2005, April 4). The relationships between heavy episodic drinking, sexual assaulting and being sexually assaulted for southern urban university students. *Electronic Journal of Human Sexuality, 8*. Retrieved from http://www.ejhs.org/volume8/heavy_drinking.htm

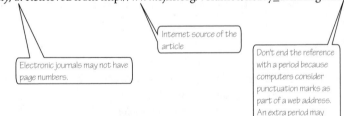

Internet source of the article

Electronic journals may not have page numbers.

Don't end the reference with a period because computers consider punctuation marks as part of a web address. An extra period may cause difficulty in accessing the article.

Reference to a journal article with more than seven authors

Halpern, D. F., Smothergill, D. W., Allen, M., Baker, S., Baum, C., Best, D., ... Weaver, K. A. (1998). Scholarship in psychology: A paradigm for the twenty-first century. *American Psychologist, 53*, 1292–1297.

> When you cite a source that includes more than seven authors, type only the first six, then add *three ellipsis points* to signify that there are other authors, then list the final author.

> Note: In the text, when there are more than seven authors, refer to them with only the first author's name followed by *et al.* (e.g., Halpern et al., 1998).

Reference for which a group is the author

> If a group has authored a paper, list the group name as the author.

> Note: The group takes the position of the author, regardless of whether the citation is online or in a traditional journal.

American Academy of Child and Adolescent Psychiatry. (2004). *Facts for families No. 10: Teen suicide.* Retrieved September 21, 2006, from www.aacap.org/publications/factsfam/suicide.htm

Reference for a special issue of a journal

> For a special issue of the journal, indicate the editor, if there is one, followed by the indication, *Ed.*, in parentheses.

> Indicate that this is a special issue, using square brackets.

Nodine, B. F. (Ed.). (1990). Psychologists teach writing [Special issue]. *Teaching of Psychology, 17*(1).

> Indicate the issue number to help the reader find the particular issue.

References Involving Books

Reference to an entire book

Petty, R. E., & Cacioppo, J. T. (1986). *Communication and persuasion: Central and peripheral routes to attitude change.* New York, NY: Springer-Verlag.

> Include the name of the city of publication and an abbreviation of the name of the state or the country of publication, followed by a colon and a space, then the publisher's name.

> Italicize book titles. Capitalize the first word of the title. If there is a subtitle following a colon, capitalize the first word after the colon.

Reference to an electronic version of a print book

Galton, F. (1892). Hereditary genius: An inquiry into its laws and consequences. Retrieved from http://www.galton.org/books/hereditary-genius/text/pdf/galton-1869-genius-v3.pdf

Internet source of the book

Reference for an edited book

Indicate the editor with *Ed.* in parentheses.
If there are multiple editors, use *Eds.*

Sternberg, R. J. (Ed.). (2000). *Guide to publishing in psychology journals.* New York, NY: Cambridge University Press.

Include the name of the city of publication and an abbreviation of the name of the state or the country of publication, followed by a colon and a space, then the publisher's name.

Reference to a chapter in a book

• Capitalize the first word of the chapter title.
• If there is a subtitle with a colon, capitalize the first word after the colon.

Kendall, P. C., Silk, J. S., & Chu, B. C. (2000). Introducing your research report: Writing the introduction. In R. J. Sternberg (Ed.), *Guide to publishing in psychology journals* (pp. 41–57). New York, NY: Cambridge.

• Give the page numbers of the chapter.
• Use the abbreviation *p.* for *page* or *pp.* for *pages.*
• The chapter title and the page information are NOT italicized.

Include the name of the city of publication and an abbreviation of the name of the state or the country of publication, followed by a colon and a space, then the publisher's name.

Identify the editor(s) of the book, with initials before the last name or names of all editors.

• Capitalize the first word of the book title.
• Italicize the book title.

Reference to a book whose author is also the publisher

> The organization is listed as the author. Put the organization name first, as if it were a typical author.

American Psychological Association. (2010). *Publication Manual of the American Psychological Association* (6th ed.). Washington, DC: Author.

> Include the name of the city of publication and an abbreviation of the name of the state or the country of publication, followed by a colon and a space, then the publisher's name.

> Instead of the publisher's name, just type the word *Author*, with the first letter capitalized.

References to Newsletters

Reference to a newsletter article with an author

Beins, B. C. (2006, November). APA style: The style we love to hate. *General Psychology Newsletter, 16*, 29–31.

> Indicate the newsletter's year of publication, followed by a comma and the month. If the exact day of the month of publication is available, include it.

Reference to a newsletter article with discontinuous pages

> Indicate the date in as much detail as listed in the newsletter.

Beins, B. C. (2005, Fall). Professional development through advanced placement psychology. *Psychology Teacher Network, 15*(3), 9, 16.

> • Italicize the publication.
> • Include the volume number.
> • Include the issue number only if the first page of each issue of the newsletter is given as page 1.

> If the article appears on discontinuous pages, indicate the pages on which the article appears.

Internet References

Reference to a multiple-page Internet site

• If there are multiple web pages on a site with no identifiable author, start with the web site's name.
• When you cite the URL, give the entry page for the web site.

If there is no date for the document, type *n.d.* to indicate "no date."

Shape Up America! (n.d.). Body fat lab. Retrieved September 1, 2006, from http://www.shapeup.org

Do NOT end the web address with a period.

Reference to a blog post

Verla (2011, April 24). There's a word for everything [Web log post]. Retrieved from http://wordswordswords.info/2011/04/24/there%E2%80%99s-a-word-for-everything/

When the author has a screen name, use it to design ate the author, even if you know the person's actual name.

Reference to an Encyclopedia Entry

If there is no author listed, put the title of the entry, which in this example is *Elisha Gray*, where the author's name usually goes.

Elisha Gray (1974). In *The Encyclopedia Britannica* (Vol. 4, p. 691). Chicago, IL: Encyclopedia Britannica.

Include the name of the city of publication and an abbreviation of the name of the state or the country of publication, followed by a colon and a space, then the publisher's name.

References to Presentations

Reference to a presentation given at a conference or other meeting

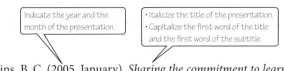

McCarthy, M., & Beins, B. C. (2005, January). *Sharing the commitment to learning: Working toward a common goal.* Paper presented at the National Institute on the Teaching of Psychology, St. Petersburg, FL.

Reference to a poster presentation given at a conference or other meeting

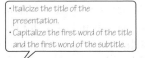

Beins, B. C. (2005, October). *Online psychological laboratory: A free resource for experiments and demonstrations.* Poster session at the Northeastern Conference for Teachers of Psychology, New Haven, CT.

Specify the conference and where it took place.

Reference to a symposium at a conference or other meeting

Indicate the year and the month.

• Do NOT italicize the title of the talk within the symposium.
• DO italicize the title of the symposium.

Weaver, K. A. (2006, August). Building community through professional development. In D. C. Appleby (Chair), *Curricular and extracurricular community-building strategies for psychology departments.* Symposium conducted at the annual convention of the American Psychological Association, New Orleans, LA.

Specify the conference and where it took place.

Insert a comma between the name of the conference and its location.

9

Final Touches
The Abstract and Formatting Details

The details are not the details. They make the design.

Charles Eames

Blue jeans are not suitable for a wedding, and a tuxedo is not suitable for a picnic. If you are going somewhere, it is probably a good idea to dress for the occasion. Likewise, after you have finished writing your paper, you need to dress it up with the finishing touches. Formatting your paper in APA style dresses it up so it fits the occasion.

In this chapter, you will learn how to assemble your APA-style research paper so that it follows the prescribed format. All APA papers follow the guidelines very closely because readers have certain expectations about what should appear in the paper and where they can find the information they want.

When you have written your Introduction, Method, Results, and Discussion sections and compiled the References section, you have finished nearly the entire substance of your manuscript. The only writing you have yet to do is the Abstract, which is a short summary of your entire paper. Once you have completed the Abstract, you should take the opportunity to review and revise your writing one final time. You should also check to see that the formatting of your paper conforms to APA style.

As you are already aware, there are more rules of APA style than you probably care to think about. You have already encountered many of them. In this chapter, though, you will learn about some of the more mechanical aspects of creating and formatting your paper in APA style.

APA Style Simplified: Writing in Psychology, Education, Nursing, and Sociology,
First Edition. Bernard C. Beins.
© 2012 John Wiley & Sons, Inc. Published 2012 by John Wiley & Sons, Inc.

The Abstract

A reader's first exposure to your writing is likely to be the Abstract, a summary of about 150 to 250 words. The Abstract is the most recently developed section of published journal articles. APA journals used to print a summary at the end of the article; authors created an abstract, but it was only used for the now-defunct *Psychological Abstracts*, which PsycINFO© replaced. Now, the Summary is gone; the Abstract fulfills the same function, but it appears at the beginning of the journal article.

Your Abstract should be a very concise description of your research question, your methodology, your results, and your conclusions. The purpose is to give the reader a quick, but good, sense of your project before reading the entire article. There are some specific elements that the Abstract should contain:

- the research question;
- the participants and subjects and their characteristics (age, sex, race/ ethnicity, number, species if nonhuman);
- the method (e.g., experimental, correlational, factor analytical), including apparatus and materials;
- the research results, including levels of statistical significance;
- conclusions and implications of your results.

When you write your Abstract, it should reflect the most important aspects of your manuscript. It should also be self-contained; that is, a reader should be able to understand everything you say without having to refer to the body of the article itself. This means defining any abbreviations you use, although you don't have to define units of measurements such as minutes, seconds, meters, and so forth.

In addition, you should use the present tense of verbs that relate to your conclusions, but past tense for describing what you did and what happened. For instance, you would write:

- The research reveals [present tense] that, on a daily basis, people are likely to be affected by subtle cues in their environment.
- The participants recalled [past tense] as many words as possible in a 5-minute period.

Also, in the Abstract, you should use active voice verbs. Passive voice verbs create uninteresting prose that may not engage your reader.

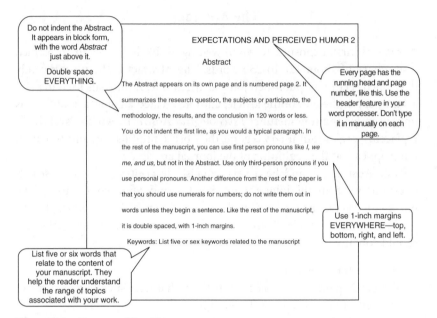

Figure 9.1   Format of the Abstract.

In final form, you should type your Abstract as a single paragraph. Don't indent the first line; the Abstract is a single block of text. An example appears in Figure 9.1.

Formatting Your Manuscript

There are a few places in your manuscript where you need to follow some specific guidelines for formatting. As you have already seen, the format of tables and figures follows pretty well-specified rules. Other sections have their own requirements, too.

Title Page

On the title page, you communicate the title of your paper, which is a pretty obvious component. You also create a running head (sometimes called a short title) that appears at the top of every page of the manuscript, including tables and figures. In previous versions of APA style, you would not have included it at the top of the pages containing figures, but in the sixth

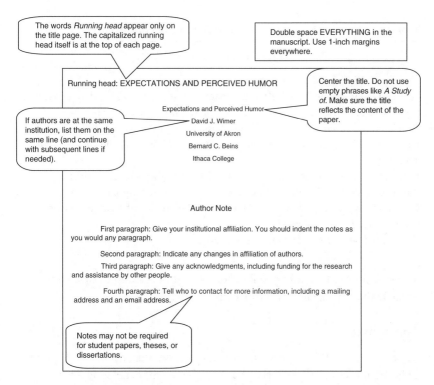

The words *Running head* appear only on the title page. The capitalized running head itself is at the top of each page.

Double space EVERYTHING in the manuscript. Use 1-inch margins everywhere.

Running head: EXPECTATIONS AND PERCEIVED HUMOR

Center the title. Do not use empty phrases like *A Study of.* Make sure the title reflects the content of the paper.

Expectations and Perceived Humor

David J. Wimer

University of Akron

Bernard C. Beins

Ithaca College

If authors are at the same institution, list them on the same line (and continue with subsequent lines if needed).

Author Note

First paragraph: Give your institutional affiliation. You should indent the notes as you would any paragraph.

Second paragraph: Indicate any changes in affiliation of authors.

Third paragraph: Give any acknowledgments, including funding for the research and assistance by other people.

Fourth paragraph: Tell who to contact for more information, including a mailing address and an email address.

Notes may not be required for student papers, theses, or dissertations.

Figure 9.2 Format of the title page. (In a manuscript submitted to a journal, notes on the title page include (a) departmental affiliation of authors, (b) changes in affiliation since the research was done, (c) acknowledgments of assistance, and (d) contact information for the authors. These may not be required for course-related manuscripts. Each of the four notes is in a separate paragraph.)

edition of the publication manual, that has changed so that the short title is on every page.

In addition, you also type the words *Running head* followed by a colon and the short title. This running head appears only in a published journal article. On the same line, in the right-hand corner, you insert the page number.

You should use your word-processing program to insert the page header. You can see a sample title page in Figure 9.2. The directions for creating the header appear in Table 9.1. You should not type in the page header and page number manually on each page. If you insert the header and page number

Table 9.1　Creating the Page Header and Page Number in Word®

Creating the page header in Word®
Click on *Insert* on the menu at the top.
Select: Header. If you check **Different Headers** for the first page and for subsequent pages, you can include the phrase *Running head:* and omit it on later pages.
Type a phrase in UPPERCASE LETTERS that gives a sense of the nature of the research, then hit the space bar a number of times to position the cursor for the page number.
In the Header and Footer bar, click on the Page Number icon and select Current Position, then Plain Number, which will insert the page number.
On the second page of the manuscript, repeat the process of creating a header without the phrase *Running head*.
Click on *Close* in the Header and Footer bar.

by hand, proper formatting will be lost any time you add or delete material because the page header will move up or down.

Appendixes

Another section that appears on occasion in a manuscript is the Appendix. This section contains material that may be of importance to readers, but more as background than as critical information for understanding the study. An appendix is likely to contain such things as stimuli used in your study, like word lists for a memory study or questionnaires that you created for your study that are not available elsewhere. Regarding questionnaires, you normally do not include them in your manuscript; instead, you give a reference that the reader can consult for details. When you have created a questionnaire yourself, it is not available elsewhere, so you can present it in an appendix.

An appendix, like everything else in your paper, is double spaced. If you have more than one appendix, each one is on its own page or pages. For a single appendix, put the word *Appendix* centered at the top of the page. (The word does not appear in italics.) When there are multiple appendixes, label them by letter (Appendix A, Appendix B, etc.)

Footnotes and Notes

In some disciplines, particularly in the humanities, footnotes are common in writing. In APA style, however, footnotes are relatively rare.

One problem with footnotes is that they interrupt the reader's attention to your ideas. The reader has to hold in memory your main point while looking to the bottom of the page for your clarification. In addition, they have to be formatted specifically for a journal article, so they are costly. Generally, if an idea is important enough to include in a footnote, it is important enough to include in the main body of text.

In some cases, footnotes are appropriate or even desirable. For example, in tables, you may include footnotes to the table if information might have to be repeated several times if you did not include the footnote. You may also include information such as probability values. You can refer to chapter 6 on presentation of notes on tables. These footnotes go immediately below the bottom rule of a table.

Table footnotes are also appropriate to indicate copyright permission. You must receive permission from a copyright holder to reproduce a table or a figure; your footnote should state where the table or figure was published, who holds the copyright, and that you have permission to use the table or figure.

If you use footnotes, number them consecutively with superscript Arabic numerals (i.e., 1, 2, etc.). The first mention of the footnote appears as follows:

The participants became irritated at being deceived,[1]

If there is any punctuation right after the word, you should almost always type the punctuation mark (e.g., comma, period) before the numeral as shown in the example above. The sole exception involves dashes; in this situation, place the numeral before the dash. When you refer to a footnote in the text, include the reference within parentheses, as follows:

the researchers made the same claim previously (see Footnote 1).

Order of Manuscript Pages

Your manuscript pages follow a prescribed order. They are numbered here for your information, but you do not number them when you type your manuscript. Not all manuscripts have each element, so you may not include all of them in a single manuscript.

When you type your paper, you begin some sections on a new page: title page, abstract, references, appendixes, author's note, footnotes, and figure captions; in addition, each table and each figure goes on its own page. On the other hand, the Method section starts on the line immediately below the end of the Introduction, the Results section starts right after the Method section, and the Discussion starts right after the Results section.

1. Title page
2. Abstract
3. Introduction
4. Method
5. Results
6. Discussion
7. References
8. Footnotes (although using your word processor's footnote capability, you can put footnotes at the bottom of the page on which you introduce them)
9. Tables
10. Figures
11. Appendices

If your manuscript presents multiple experiments, you may need to repeat elements 4, 5, and 6 for each study. If so, you include a section called *General Discussion* to summarize and integrate all the studies you conducted.

Section Headings

In APA style, there are five different styles for heading sections of the manuscript. Many single-study manuscripts use two of them, levels 1 and 2. The levels and how you type them appear in Table 9.2, with schematic examples

Table 9.2 Different Levels of Headings in an APA-style Manuscript

Level	Format
Level	*Format*
Level 1	**Centered in Bold with the First Letter of Important Words Capitalized**
Level 2	**Flush Left in Bold with the First Letter of Important Words Capitalized**
Level 3	**Indented in bold with only the first letter of the first word capitalized, ending with a period.** Begin body text after the period.
Level 4	***Indented in bold and italicized with only the first letter of the first word capitalized, ending with a period.*** Begin body text after the period.
Level 5	*Indented, but NOT in bold, and italicized with only the first letter of the first word capitalized, ending with a period.* Begin body text after the period.

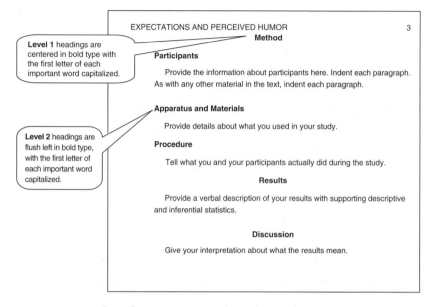

Figure 9.3   Headings for manuscripts with two levels of headings.

in Figures 9.3. 9.4, and 9.5. With a slightly more complicated manuscript that has more subsections, you may need more than two levels of headings. Figure 9.5 shows how you might use all five levels of headings.

Miscellaneous Formatting Details

There are specific formatting guidelines that appear fairly trivial; they are easy to overlook, though. The rules cited in this chapter involve the common elements of formatting. For the formatting of less common elements, you can refer to the APA *Publication Manual* (2010).

There are specific rules regarding capitalization. Some of them are entirely consistent with the writing style that you probably already use. But some are rather specific to APA style. Examples appear in Table 9.3.

There are other specific points in APA style regarding formatting. They include the use of italics, appropriate use of abbreviations, and creating series within text. The rules and examples are illustrated in Tables 9.4, 9.5, and 9.6, respectively.

One further element of presentation involves quotations. There are two relevant types of quotations for our purposes: direct and indirect. A direct quotation is the kind most people recognize: You use the exact words of

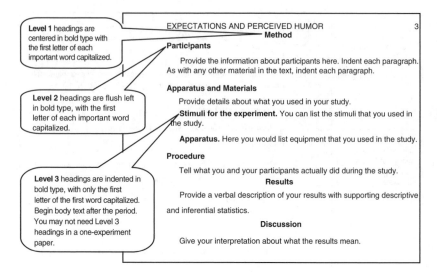

Figure 9.4   Headings for a manuscript with three levels of headings.

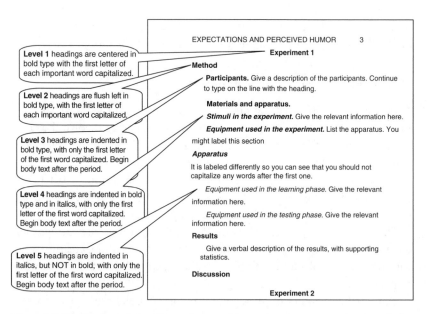

Figure 9.5   Levels of headings for multiexperiment manuscripts and for manuscripts with all five levels of headings.

Table 9.3 Capitalization in APA Style

Rule	Example
Capitalize the first word in a sentence.	
Capitalize the first word after a colon if it starts a full sentence but not otherwise.	• There are many rules: Capitalization [*This is the first word after a colon; it starts a full sentence*] can be confusing. • This table presents guidance on a frequently problematic element of writing: capitalization. [*This word does not start a full sentence, so you do not capitalize it.*]
Capitalize important words in titles of books and journal articles, in figure captions, and titles of tables.	• At the bookstore, the writing student bought *Sister Bernadette's Barking Dog: The Quirky History and Lost Art of Diagramming Sentences* [After the colon, *The* is capitalized, but *and* and *of* are not because they are not important words in the title.]
Capitalize the name of sections of the manuscript when you refer to them in the body of the paper.	• The details appear in the Results section.
Capitalize names of departments in a college or university if the proper name is used, but not if the name is used generically.	• He joined the Department of Psychology. • She became a psychology major.
Capitalize nouns that are followed by numbers.	• He memorized List 3 in Experiment 2.
Do not capitalize nouns that: • describe common elements of books and tables, even if they are followed by numbers; • precede a variable;	 • You can refer to Table 3 in chapter 7 [a *chapter is a common element of a book*] for information on misuse of contractions in writing; specific examples are in column 1 [*a column is a common part of a table*]. • This participant was in the high-anxiety condition. There was no effect of the anxiety variable [anxiety *is the name of the variable; high-anxiety is the name of the specific condition*].

(*Continued*)

Table 9.3 *(cont'd)*

Rule	Example
• are names of effects, conditions, or variables in a study.	
Capitalize variable names that accompany multiplication signs, as with interaction effects.	• There was a Sex × Humor interaction. [*Normally, do not capitalize sex or humor because they are variable names, but they appear with a multiplication sign, so they are capitalized in this case.*]
Do not capitalize the multiplication sign in an interaction effect.	
Capitalize the genus, but not the species, of animals.	• *Drosophila melanogaster*. [*Note that the genus (Drosophila) and species (melanogaster) appear in italics.*]

Table 9.4 Italics in APA Style

Rule	Example
Do not routinely use italics to create emphasis; use syntax for emphasis.	*Incorrect*: The high-expectation condition was the *only* condition in which an effect emerged. *Better*: The sole condition in which we found an effect was the high-expectation condition. [*Moving the main point to the beginning of the sentence may focus the reader's attention on that point.*]
You may use italics if, by not doing so, a reader might misunderstand the word.	The *exhausted* group slowed down. [*If you were studying the effects of fatigue, you could use italics to indicate that this is the name of a specific group, not merely that the participants were tired.*]
Use italics when you are referring to a word as a specific word rather than in its usual meaning.	He crossed out the word *before* before he crossed out the word *after*. [*The meaning of the first before, in italics, refers to the word, not to the concept of time. If you didn't italicize before, the sentence would appear*

Table 9.4 (*cont'd*)

Rule	Example
	ungrammatical and would confuse the reader. In speech, we use pauses and emphasis to differentiate the meanings.]
If you are using italics and are going to include a word or phrase that would normally be italicized, such as a book title, switch to Roman type (i.e., do not use italics).	*The speaker relied heavily on Freud's book* Dora: An Analysis of a Case of Hysteria *in the assessment of psychoanalysis.* [*Book titles are normally italicized; in this example, it is in Roman type because the wording around it is in italics.*]
Use italics for: • titles of books and journals;	*Psychological Science, Journal of Experimental Psychology: General*
• the volume number in a journal you cite;	*Psychological Science, 17* [*volume 17 of the journal*], 568–571
• scales on tests;	Scales on the Guilford–Zimmerman Temperament Survey: G (*General*), R (*Restraint*)
• identification of genus, species, and variety of animals.	*Drosophila melanogaster*
Use italics for statistical tests and for indicating probability, but do not use italics for subscripts in statistical expressions.	$t(25) = 1.10, p > .05$ $M_{women} = 3.82$ [*The letter M, representing the mean, is italicized, but the subscript indicating the group is not.*]
Use italics for anchors in a rating scale.	The participants rated their sense of humor on a scale of 1 (*poor*) to 7 (*good*).

another person and enclose those words within quotation marks. Indirect quotations refer to the expression of somebody else's idea, but not the exact words. For either type, you need to cite and give credit to the person. Table 9.7 shows how to format quotations in APA style.

Direct quotations are relatively rare in psychological writing. The most common use is when another author has made specific points that relate closely to your ideas. Shorter quotations appear within the text like any other material. Longer quotations are set apart from the rest of the text, in a block; they do not make use of quotations marks. When you use quotations,

Table 9.5 Abbreviations in APA Style

Rule	Example
Do not use abbreviations: • if they will distract the reader from your point; • if they seldom appear after the first time you introduce them; • for variables and conditions if the abbreviation will not be clear to the reader.	The IVs and DVs included RTs after lesioning of the LH and VMH. [*Instead, consider writing out some of the abbreviations that might not be obvious to a reader.*]
For the first use of an abbreviation, write out the term in full, followed by the abbreviation in parentheses.	The parents' socioeconomic status (SES) accounted for some variability in children's educational attainment.
Abbreviations are acceptable when that is the typical way people write them, including state names .	IQ, AIDS; but write out new or relatively rare terms for the first presentation: Emotional Quotient (EQ) or NY for New York, AL for Alabama.
Use abbreviations derived from Latin (e.g., for example; i.e., that is; &, and) only in parentheses.	The high-stress group (i.e., those exposed to the cold-pressor test) showed anxiety. [*i.e. is a Latin abbreviation for* id est, *meaning* that is.]
Use an English variation of the Latin phrase when it appears in the main body of the text. Exceptions: • Use the Latin "et al." (meaning *and others*) in references even when the reference is not in parentheses. • Use the ampersand (&) in the reference list before the final name when there is more than one author.	The high-stress group—that is, those exposed to the cold-pressor test—showed anxiety.
Do not abbreviate some measures of time because the abbreviations might confuse the reader.	• day (not d.) • week (not wk.) • month (not mo.) • year (not yr.)
Use periods with abbreviations for: • initials in people's names;	• A. Lincoln, H. M. [*a means of concealing a person's identity, as in the case of H. M., who lost the ability to form new memories*]

Table 9.5 *(cont'd)*

Rule	Example
• Latin abbreviations; • abbreviations in references.	• et al. • Supp. [for *Supplement*]
Do not use periods for: • abbreviations of state or country names; • acronyms using capital letters; • common measurements that you abbreviate. Exception: Use a period for abbreviating inch (in.) because otherwise, a reader could confuse it with the preposition *in*.	• USA [United States], UK [United Kingdom], OH [Ohio] • APA, APS, CIA, FBI • ft [foot], m [meter], cm [centimeter] • The line was 5 in. from beginning to end.
To render an abbreviation plural, add the letter *s*. Do Do NOT use an apostrophe. Exceptions: • Do not make an abbreviation unit of measurement plural; keep it singular. • Make the abbreviation for the word *page* plural by adding a second p and a period.	RTs (reaction times) 5 m [*for specifying 5 meters; do not use 5 ms*) pp. 28–59 [*To indicate pages 28 to 59 in a book chapter, use pp. rather than ps.*]

Table 9.6 Creating Series in APA Style

Rule	Example
Creating a series of elements in the main body of text involves lowercase letters within parentheses. Note: Use complete parentheses, (a), not just the close-parentheses symbol, a).	Correct: Use 1-inch margins for (a) the top, (b) the bottom, (c) the right, and (d) the left edges of the page. Incorrect: Use 1-inch margins for a) the top, b) the bottom, c) right, and d) left edges of the page.
In a series, use commas to separate the different elements.	Correct: Use 1-inch margins for (a) the top, (b) the bottom, (c) right, and (d) left edges of the page.
Exception: Use semicolons to separate elements in the series if there are commas within one or more series.	Correct: The symbols were (a) blue, green, and red; (b) orange and yellow; or (c) black and white.
If your series is a listing of paragraphs, use an arabic (not roman) numeral followed by a period. Do not use parentheses. You may also use bullets (•) if numbering paragraphs suggests that the specific order of points is important when that is not your intent.	The participants completed three tasks: 1. They completed a survey. This segment involved … 2. They identified the reasons for their choices. This task was open-ended … 3. They decided which task they enjoyed the most. They indicated this by …

Table 9.7 Using Quotations in APA Style

Rule	Example
Direct quotations	
For quotations, always cite the author's (or authors') name, the year of publication, and the pages on which the quotation appeared. For electronic materials, paragraph numbers may replace page numbers. Place this information right after the quotation.	
• If the quotation is in the middle of a sentence, put the citation within parentheses immediately after the quotation. Do not use any punctuation not required for the structure of the sentence.	We know that "poor writing habits are exceedingly difficult to unlearn" (Sommer, 2006, p. 956) once they are ingrained.
• If the quotation ends a sentence, put the citation information within parentheses; put the sentence-ending period after the citation.	We know that "poor writing habits are exceedingly difficult to unlearn" (Sommer, 2006, p. 956).
• If the quotation is part of a blocked paragraph, put the citation within parentheses after the final punctuation mark.	Mentors of most graduate students usually train their students in rules of academic style. Writing for the public requires specific training as well. (Sommer, 2006, p. 957)
A quotation is almost always reproduced exactly as it appeared originally, even if there are errors in the original. If there is an error that might confuse a reader, insert [sic], using square brackets, immediately after the error. *Sic* is a word that writers use to inform readers of the presence of errors. It is Latin for "thus" or "so."	If a writer had incorrectly used *there* instead of *their* in a sentence, you would use the incorrect spelling: • The children went to there [sic] homes after school.

Exceptions:
If a quotation could confuse a reader because the context of the words is not present, you may add clarifying words by inserting them [within square brackets].

A sentence out of context may be missing material needed for understanding it. You may add words to preserve the meaning:

- Participants in [the treatment group] were not aware of the manipulation.

You may shorten a quotation by eliminating unnecessary words and inserting three periods (…) to indicate ellipsis. Place a space before and after each period. If a sentence ends immediately before the ellipsis, include the period at the end of that sentence, meaning that you have four periods.

The results reveal that … anxiety is associated with poor performance. Mortality salience generates thoughts of death. … Participants high in neuroticism were especially vulnerable. (*The missing material comes after the end of a sentence, so you need a period to end the sentence; then you insert the three ellipsis points.*)

You may add emphasis by italicizing material in a quotation: Italicize the words to be emphasized and indicate this in square brackets with "[italics added]." If material is italicized in the original, indicate this fact by writing in square brackets "[italics in original]."

If you want to emphasize certain words in a quotation, you may italicize them, indicating that the italics are yours:

- The children went to their homes *after school* [italics added].

For quotations of 40 words or fewer, enclose the quotation within "double quotation marks" in the text.
For quotations longer than 40 words, create a block paragraph. The block's margins should be indented five spaces on the left and right relative to the main body of text. Do NOT use quotation marks.

If there is a second quotation within a short quotation, enclose that second quotation within single quotation marks.
If there is a second quotation within a long quotation, enclose that second quotation within double quotation marks.

"The participant said 'I have to leave now' before the experiment had ended."

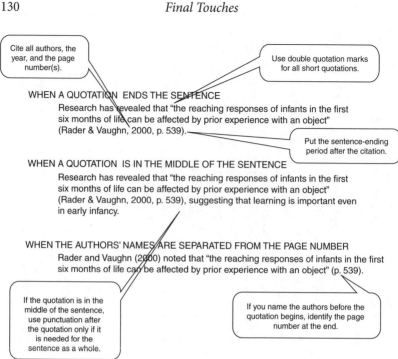

Figure 9.6 Illustration of format of short quotations of 40 words or fewer.

you need to identify the source, including the page number, in the text. Examples of how to format short quotations appear in Figure 9.6, based on research by Rader and Vaughn (2000).

Sometimes you may include a long quotation (i.e., more than 40 words) in your writing. In such a case, you create a separate paragraph in block form and indent five spaces on both left and right margins relative to the rest of the text. As with all other parts of the manuscript, you use double spacing for this block paragraph. You do not indent the first line of the paragraph, but if the quotation is more than one paragraph, you indent the second and succeeding paragraphs. An example of the style for a long quotation appears in Figure 9.7. If you were writing about perceptions of a just world, you might cite the research by DePalma, Madey, Tillman, and Wheeler (2000), as indicated in the figure.

Indirect quotations present another writer's ideas, but you may change the wording slightly or extensively. As such, you should attribute the work to the other person, but APA style does not mandate including numbers of

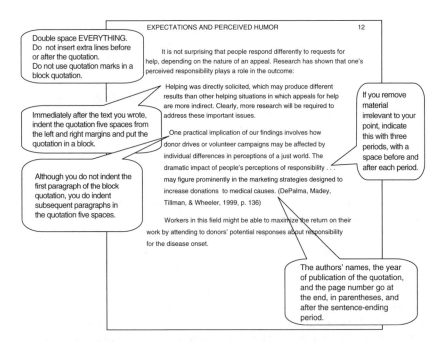

Figure 9.7 Illustration of format of long quotations of 40 words or more. The quotation is indented in its entirety. The first part of the quotation is not indented, but subsequent paragraphs in the quotation are indented.

the pages on which those ideas had appeared, although it is desirable. An indirect quotation does not look any different than the rest of the body of your text.

Finally, there are certain conventions regarding punctuation marks. Some commonly used punctuation marks and guidelines for their use are given in Table 9.8. Remember that there are other, infrequently used, rules that are part of APA style. You can refer to the *Publication Manual* if you have additional questions.

Final Touches

Table 9.8   Using Common Punctuation Marks

Rule	*Example*
Comma	
Use a comma between elements in a series, including before the word *and* or *or*, that separates the second last and the last element in the series.	The flag was red, white, and blue. Note: In some writing styles, one would not insert a comma after white, but in APA style, the comma is appropriate.
Use a comma to separate independent clauses. Independent clauses can stand alone as sentences.	He remembered the names, but he forgot the addresses.
Do not use a comma to separate two parts of a compound predicate.	He remembered the names but forgot the addresses.
Use a comma to separate a nonrestrictive clause (i.e., one that is not necessary for the meaning of the sentence and that only provides additional information) from the rest of the sentence.	The stimulus, which appeared in the center of the screen, remained visible for 300 msec. Note: The material in the clause beginning with *which* is not necessary for the meaning of the sentence. Such clauses are introduced by the conjunction *which*
Do not use a comma to separate a restrictive clause (i.e., one that is necessary for the meaning of the sentence) from the rest of the sentence.	The stimulus that followed the rest period remained visible for 300 msec. Note: The material in the clause beginning with *that* is necessary for the reader to understand the point of the sentence. Such clauses are introduced by the conjunction *that*.
Use a comma in citing a specific date. Do not use a comma for nonspecific dates	February 27, 1980 February 1980
Use a comma to separate the year in a citation from other elements.	(Rader & Vaughn, 2000)
Use a comma to group large numbers by thousands.	9,876,543

Table 9.8 (*cont'd*)

Rule	Example
Exceptions: Do not use commas:	
• to separate numbers to the right of the decimal place;	1,234.4891
• when reporting temperatures or acoustic measurements;	1500°C or 1000 Hz
• for degrees of freedom.	$r(1250) = .03, p > .05$
Semicolon	
Use a semicolon to separate two independent clauses that can stand alone as sentences but that are not separated by a conjunction such as *and*, *or*, or *but*.	The participant recalled the words; she also completed the questionnaire.
Use a semicolon to separate components within a series if some components make use of commas	The participant completed the informed consent form, the questionnaire, and the callback form; read the stimulus materials; and recalled the main points from the passage.
Parentheses	
Use parentheses to indicate publication dates.	Smith (2004) found that …
Use parentheses for identifying pages on which quotations had appeared.	"… was not apparent" (p. 303).
Use parentheses to create a series of elements.	(a) lines, (b) circles, and (c) squares
Use parentheses the first time you present an abbreviation.	We recorded the participant's reaction time (RT).
Do not use parentheses within parentheses. Instead, use square brackets.	(The analysis of variance [ANOVA] revealed that …) Note: Use the square brackets within parenthetical material.
Do not use parentheses to present statistical results. Readers may have trouble processing multiple levels of parentheses.	Incorrect: The effect was nonsignificant, ($t(25) = 1.02, p > .05$).

(*Continued*)

Table 9.8   *(cont'd)*

Rule	Example
Hyphens	
Hyphenate a compound adjective if it could be misunderstood by the reader if you did not use the hyphen.	The governor released the details of a public-health issue. Note: Without the hyphen, it is not clear whether the issue involved public health (e.g., the outbreak of a disease) or an issue about the governor's health that had been made public and that he wanted to clarify.
Hyphenate an adjective–noun combination when it precedes a noun that it modifies.	He was said to have an anal-retentive personality.
Do not hyphenate an adjective–noun combination if it does not precede a noun.	His personality was anal retentive.

10

Creating Poster Presentations

Words and pictures can work together to communicate more powerfully than either alone.

William Albert Allard

Have you ever been trapped at a lecture that seemed to last forever? And you could not find a way to leave without being noticed? Too many students have had that experience in their classes, and too many researchers have had the same feeling at conference presentations. Fortunately, there is a solution to a boring talk that has way too many words. The solution is to replace the talk with a picture that is worth a thousand words.

Many conferences have poster sessions that capture your attention with lively visual presentations. You can see at a glance what a research project is about. And, if it doesn't interest you, you can just walk away.

The goal in a poster presentation is to create a compelling visual representation of your project. Poster sessions have become a common feature at scientific meetings because a large number of people can display their work and discuss it with others in a face-to-face setting. There may be dozens or even hundreds of posters in an area, depending on the size of a conference. People can walk by the posters and, if a topic catches their eye, talk to the researcher individually.

Differentiating Visual and Written Communication

In previous chapters, I have discussed ways to optimize your writing for maximal effect. A poster has a very different orientation than a written

APA Style Simplified: Writing in Psychology, Education, Nursing, and Sociology,
First Edition. Bernard C. Beins.
© 2012 John Wiley & Sons, Inc. Published 2012 by John Wiley & Sons, Inc.

paper. In a traditional manuscript, you include important details for the reader to assess. In fact, it is almost the case that you cannot provide too many details in a manuscript. On the other hand, a poster will suffer if you try to include too much information.

The reason for this difference is that a reader can spend as much time on a manuscript as desired. The person can refer to earlier material and check out detail for fuller understanding. A poster session is a more fluid experience. People walk back and forth, look at posters, and approach some posters in order to talk with the presenter. In this forum, there are multiple posters to view and multiple presenters to approach. A poster that has a lot of detail often requires a lot of text. Most of the time, people don't want to spend lots of time reading through minute detail on a poster. Instead, they want to find out about the major points. If they have questions about details, they can talk with the presenter. Consequently, when you create a poster, you should figure out the four or five most important points that you want to convey, then convey them simply and accurately.

The details of organizing a poster are still evolving as the technology for creating them changes. Your poster may consist of perhaps a dozen or so individual sheets or it may be a single large sheet. In either case, visitors to your poster are going to be more receptive if it is easy for them to understand what you are communicating and if it is visually attractive.

Reducing the Amount of Information

Most posters retain the general format of an APA-style manuscript, although there is no need to pay as close attention to the details of APA style in a poster. You will still need an Introduction, a Method section, a Results section, and a Discussion section. But the exact format relies on your judgment as to what points are most critical to you.

As a rule, people at a poster session tend to walk slowly along the line of posters, glancing at the title of the presentation, then at the layout of information. If the topic is of interest, a person might glance at what seem to be the major points illustrated on the poster. If those points are hard to discern, the person will walk away. What this means is that the most important points of your poster should leap out at a viewer. If your ideas are presented clearly and simply, the person may stop and talk to you about your work.

There are always important points that you cannot include in your poster because of space limitations and because of the need not to overwhelm a potentially interested viewer. You can discuss these details in a face-to-face conversation or in a handout. But if you try to include them all on your poster, the results will be unsatisfactory to you and to the viewer.

An effective poster presents enough information to get the viewer's interest without presenting so much that the person simply walks away.

Visual Style

Most of the time, people at poster sessions need to view your work from a distance. Thus, your message should be clearly legible from a distance of 3–4 feet away. There are no hard and fast rules about the font size you should use in creating your poster, but it is fairly typical to see 48-point fonts for the title of the poster, 36-point fonts for major section headings, and 18- to 24-point fonts for the main body of the poster.

Generally, presenters are allotted a space as small as 3 × 4 ft (1 × 1.3 m) or as large as 4 × 6 ft (1.3 × 2 m). You should always look through the conference material so you know how much space you will have. As you put your poster together, it will seem that there is too little room for everything you want to say. Don't succumb to the temptation to pack in a lot of text in order to make the points you think are important. Limit yourself to the most critical points.

Many people recommend creating a light background with dark lettering. A stark contrast between dark letters and a light background makes viewing easier. On the other hand, a dark background with light lettering may initially attract attention, but viewers can find it tiring to read for long.

Figure 10.1 shows one example of a poster that a student and I presented at the annual convention of the Eastern Psychological Association. It appeared on a single large sheet. You can see how it follows the general approach of an APA-style paper, with an introduction consisting of the basic research questions, the methodology, the results, and the discussion. What differs in a poster is that the amount of information is considerably less than in a traditional manuscript.

This example offers only one possibility regarding how to present information; you can tailor your own poster to fit your style and needs. For example, if you are allotted a large amount of space, you can present more information; if your space is smaller, you need to reduce the amount of information. You might also add, remove, or rearrange the various visual elements. Furthermore, you can use color, boxes, or bold type to highlight important information.

If you do not have the capability of producing a large, single-sheet poster, you can still create an attractive poster. The positioning of the various sections of the poster (i.e., Introduction, Method, Results, Discussion) is likely to resemble that in Figures 10.2 and 10.3.

Sense of Humor:
Alycia Ippolito &
Ithaca

Abstract

People attribute certain personality characteristics to others, depending on the perceived sense of humor of those others. In this study, we investigated whether participants would attribute the same characteristics to themselves that previous research has shown that they attribute to others. The results revealed that personality stereotypes associated with others show some similarity to self-reported traits. In addition, contrary to numerous claims, people can accurately indicate their relative level of sense of humor.

Basic Questions

1. Do people assess the relation between their personalities and humor as they assess that relation in others?[2]
2. Can people accurately report their level of sense of humor in relation to others?[1, 4, 5]

Method

Participants

65 undergraduates volunteered

43 women, 22 men

Stimuli

Multidimensional Sense of Humor Scale (MDSHS)[6, 7]
Neuroticism, Extraversion, Openness, Conscientiousness, and Agreeableness Scales[3]

Procedure

Participants completed the MDSHS to obtain an objective measure of sense of humor.
Participants completed self-report scales to measure level of factors on the Five-Factor Model of Personality: Extraversion, Neuroticism, Agreeableness, Conscientiousness, and Openness.
Testing occurred in groups or individually online.

Sense of Humor Scale

Characteristics

The MDSHS revealed subcomponents of personality:
• Social uses of humor
• Production of humor
• Using humor for coping
• Negative attitude toward humor

Sense of Humor and Funniness

Participants self-rated on:
• How funny they thought they were
• Their level of sense of humor
• Do they recognize the humor in most jokes?

Results

Personality and Sense of Humor

Does low sense of humor reveal high neuroticism?

Previous research[2] identified an inverse relation between sense of humor in hypothetical others (stereotypes of others) and their neuroticism.

Our research reveals a similar, but marginal, negative relation between a person's self-reported levels of humor and level of neuroticism, $r(63) = -.208, p = .096$.

Do extraverted people show high levels of sense of humor?

People with high level of sense of humor show high levels of humor production, but not overall sense of humor.

This finding matches stereotypes reported in earlier research.[2] The stereotype of extraverted people who are humorous has some validity, $r(63) = .418, p < .001$.

Figure 10.1 Example of a single-sheet poster for presentation at a conference.

Are We All Above Average?
Bernard C. Beins
College

Results

Do openness to experience and agreeableness relate to humor?

People with high scores on these traits show greater appreciation of humor, $r(63) = .258$, $p = .038$ and $r(63) = .391$, $p = .001$, respectively, but not production or coping. These findings replicates earlier research on stereotypes of others.[2]

Do we know how funny we are?

Previous claims: people don't know their SoH[1, 5, 6] but rate themselves highly.

People are reluctant to rate themselves as low in humor. But MSHS score for humor production relates to self-reported level of funniness, $r(63) = .518$, $p < .001$, and self-reported SoH correlates with MSHS score, $r(63) = .547$, $p < .001$.

People know their humor competence and report it veridically: Not everybody is above average.

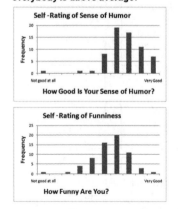

Self-Rating of Sense of Humor
How Good Is Your Sense of Humor?

Self-Rating of Funniness
How Funny Are You?

Results

Self-Rating of Humor Recognition
How Good Are You at Getting Jokes?

Participants differentiated between how funny they are $(M = 7.7)$ and what was their level of sense of humor $(M = 6.6)$, $F(1, 63) = 31.295$, $p < .001$.

Conclusions

When people relate their own personality traits and sense of humor, they generate a similar pattern of results to when they rate hypothetical others, suggesting that stereotypes about personality and humor have some validity.

Some of the Big Five personality traits are reliably associated with dimensions of humor in theoretically predictable ways.

Contrary to previous reports[1, 3, 4] we have seen, people can place themselves accurately on a continuum of how funny they are. Lower sense of humor is associated with lower self-ratings of humor; high sense of humor is associated with higher self-ratings.

References

1. Allport, G. W. (1961). *Pattern and grown in personality*. New York: Holt, Rinehart, and Winston.
2. Cann, A., & Calhoun, L. G., (2001). Perceived personality associations with differences in sense of humor: Stereotypes of hypothetical others with high or low senses of humor. *Humor, 14*, 117–130.
3. Fine, G. A. (1975). Components of perceived sense of humor ratings of self and others. *Psychological Reports, 36*, 793–794.
4. International Personality Item Pool (2001). A scientific collaboratory for the development of advanced measures of personality traits and other individual differences. Retrieved April 17, 2006 from http://ipip.ori.org.
5. Kruger, J., & Dunning, d. (1999). Unskilled and unaware of it: How difficulties in recognizing one's own incompetence lead to inflated self-assessments. *Journal of Personality and Social Psychology, 77*, 1121–1134.
6. Lefcourt, . H. M., & Martin, R. A. (1986). *Humor and life stress: Antidote to adversity*. New York: Springer/Verlag.
7. Thorson, J. A., & Powell, F. C. (1993). Development and validation of a multidimensional sense of humor scale. *Journal of Clinical Psychology, 49*, 13–23.
8. Thorson, J. A., & Powell, F. C. (1993). Sense of humor and dimensions of personality. *Journal of Clinical Psychology, 49*, 799–809.

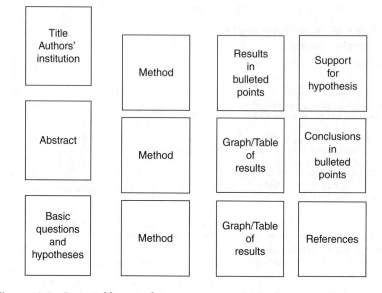

Figure 10.2 Potential layout of a poster using multiple sheets of paper.

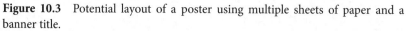

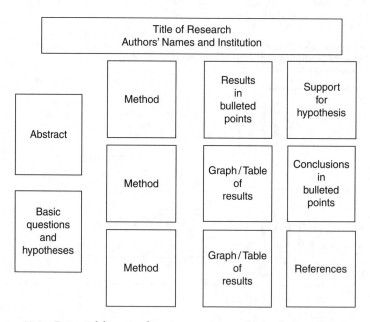

Figure 10.3 Potential layout of a poster using multiple sheets of paper and a banner title.

These figures illustrate how you can create a poster with multiple sheets of paper. In Figure 10.2, the title and authors' names are on a standard sheet of paper. In Figure 10.3, the title and authors' names appear on a banner spanning the top of the poster. In the latter version, you would need to type several sheets of paper with partial information, then cut and paste them together so they look like a single long sheet.

For such a display, you can group related information (e.g., all the material for the Method section) together spatially simply by placing the sheets in proximity to one another. It is also possible to use color to group them. Presenters often use a slightly larger, colored sheet of paper behind the standard white paper to create a colored border to make the pages stand out. The use of two or three different colors can give the viewer a sense of which pages go together. Laminating the pages can also enhance your poster's attractiveness and make it easy to carry without damaging it.

In terms of the flow of information on your poster, a top-to-bottom and left-to-right progression is sensible. People are used to reading in that direction, so when they peruse your poster, they are likely to start at the top left and move down to the bottom, going up to your second column of information, then down again, and so on.

It is common in the first part of the poster that the statement of the basic questions has replaced a traditional Introduction section. If your research was a follow-up to some previous study, you can cite that research, but you generally omit all but the most important background information. Further, sometimes the references are not in traditional APA style in the introductory part of the poster. That format would take up too much precious space on the poster.

Similarly, the Method section is very much reduced compared with a standard research report. For a poster, all you need to do is highlight the general nature of the participants, materials, and procedure. One space-saving technique is to include a photograph of any apparatus, which can replace a written description. If a viewer wants more detail, you are there to provide that information; a handout is also helpful for presenting the specifics.

The Results section benefits greatly from graphics. Figures allow a viewer to get the gist of the results easily. A bulleted presentation of the main points is effective in directing the viewer's attention to critical information. It helps the viewers if you do not force them to do a lot of searching to find your major points. A handout can provide an elaboration of the basic sketch that appears on the poster.

Finally, the conclusions can be simple, bulleted points, without much elaboration or context. This simple approach would not work for a full-length research report, but it gives the viewer a good idea of what you concluded.

You should keep in mind that these examples are just suggestions. If you need more space to explain your hypotheses, you should take it and, perhaps, reduce the amount of space you devote to the methodology. The most important point is that you convey the message you want the reader to get. It doesn't matter exactly how you do it, as long as you manage to do it.

Your Behavior: The Ethic of a Poster Session

Attire

A poster session may be your first public and professional activity. You want to make a good impression. As such, some types of clothing are appropriate, but others are not. It isn't unreasonable to consider a poster session as a type of interview. For instance, just as viewers judge the quality of your research, at least in part, from the layout of your poster, they will judge your credibility by the way you look. You should dress as a professional. This means dressing so a person responds to your work rather than to the way you look. You might object to the idea that people will evaluate your work based on how you look, but that is reality.

What constitutes professional attire varies depending on the individual and the venue. At some professional conferences, some presenters wear formal, business attire while others are more casual. At student conferences, it is more the norm for presenters to dress in "business casual" clothing.

For women, a business suit would never be inappropriate, but it is probably more than you need. Instead, slacks or skirts are usually acceptable. As a rule, a conservative approach to colors is more professional than flashy or trendy colors. Thus, slacks or skirts that are black, brown, khaki, navy blue, or other traditional colors will help you make a good impression. A blouse or shirt should coordinate with your slacks or skirt. It is probably best to avoid fabrics such as velour or velvet, denim, or party-wear fabrics.

Your shoes should have a professional appearance, so it would not be appropriate to wear extremely casual sandals, high heels or platform shoes. At the same time, you should wear comfortable shoes. Poster sessions last for 1–2 hr. Attractive but painful shoes can detract greatly from your experience.

Men have less latitude than women regarding professional attire. It's generally a business suit, which is acceptable but probably more than you need, or a sport coat with appropriate slacks. Depending on the specific meeting, you may be expected to wear a tie. Men should wear leather (or synthetic leather) shoes, not athletic shoes.

You may find it interesting that essentially no research has been devoted to what constitutes an effective poster. Many people have proposed guidelines that others have adopted. But the elements of a successful poster are as much a matter of art, tradition, and consensus as anything else.

On the other hand, a team of two researchers has investigated the effect of the clothing of a poster presenter on attention paid to the poster. Keegan and Bannister (2003) discovered that when a presenter's blouse was color coordinated to match the color of her poster, there were more visitors to the poster than when her clothes clashed with the poster.

Covering Your Poster

Poster sessions generally run for 1–2 hr, during which time people expect you to be at your poster. Your research is more interesting to you than to anybody else, so don't be discouraged if quite a few people glance your way and move on without talking to you about your work. In fact, many more people will bypass your poster than will actually stop and talk about it with you. The value of a poster session is that it allows people with similar interests to interact individually; those with other interests can find different posters.

It can be frustrating to watch people walk by, but that is the nature of a poster session. Also, if you stand right in front of your poster, you may block the view of your work, so you should stand slightly to one side.

This doesn't mean that you can't talk to the person whose poster is next to yours or to your friends and coauthors. But it does mean that when an interested viewer approaches, he or she should feel comfortable talking to you. If you are engaged in an animated conversation with a friend, the viewer may not want to interrupt you.

When you are discussing your research, somebody may ask a question that you can't answer. It is acceptable to say you don't know the answer, but you should try to address the issue that was raised.

It also helps to have a handout for people who are interested. The handout could be a small copy of your poster or it could be an APA-style manuscript describing your research. People can talk to you about your work, then study it in greater depth at a later point. Very often there are chairs at poster session on which you can place your handouts so people don't have to ask you for one. Or you could affix a large envelope containing your handouts on the poster board.

Finally, one of the drawbacks to a poster session is that, if you are at your poster, you may not have a lot of time to walk around and view those of others. One remedy is to set up your poster before your session begins, then to walk around the poster area to see what is there; if others have handouts, you can pick them up. Another possibility is to wait until the crowd in the poster session diminishes before you look at other posters. At this point in the poster session, you may have formed a relationship with the person at the poster next to yours; that person can tell any viewers that you will be right back. If you have a coauthor on the poster, you can take turns standing at the poster and walking around the display area.

The keys to a successful poster presentation are (a) spending time in advance creating a visually compelling poster with substantial content, (b) being familiar with the work so you can answer questions about it, (c) being comfortable telling people what you know, and (d) adopting a professional demeanor as you interact with viewers.

Creating Your Poster Using PowerPoint®

Creating attractive posters using PowerPoint® is fairly easy. There are some basic steps you can use whether your poster will consist of a single, large sheet or multiple, standard sheets.

Once you begin working with PowerPoint®, you will see that most of the mechanical steps associated with creating your poster are relatively straightforward. The most challenging aspects include (a) presenting the content in a clear and compelling way and (b) generating an effective visual layout.

Regarding the visual layout, you may be able to get some guidance from people who have already created posters. Look at their products and take your cues from them. If you have attended previous poster sessions, you may be able to remember what aspects of the posters you found interesting and what aspects you avoided.

You can begin developing your poster by following the steps outlined in Table 10.1. At many points along the way, you will have to make choices. Remember that none of the choices is irrevocable. If you decide you do not like the effect, you can undo it and substitute another.

Table 10.1 Initial steps for Creating a Large, Single-Sheet Poster Presentation Using PowerPoint®

What you want to do	*How to do it*	*The result*
Set up the poster.	Select *Design* on the toolbar and choose *Page Setup* → *Custom* → *Landscape*.	This lets you specify the size of the poster.
	• Identify the height and width of your poster. Then in the box that asks for the number of slides, select *1*.	Make sure you check the conference information about how much space you will have for your poster. Do not exceed the dimensions of the allotted space.
View all or part of your poster.	On the toolbar indicating percentage of poster to display, select *View* → *Fit to Window* to see how the entire poster looks.	When you select *View* → *Fit to Window*, you will be able to see the overall layout, how much space you have used, and how much space you still have. You will not be able to read the text very well.
	Select another percentage for a partial view of the poster. If you select 25%, you will see only one quarter of the poster, but you will be able to work with it more easily.	When you select a specific percentage of the poster, the larger the percentage, the more of the total poster you will be able to see.
Display lines to guide poster creation.	Select *View* on the toolbar and check *Gridlines*.	This will put lines on the poster so you can align different parts of the poster neatly. The lines that appear here will not appear on your poster.

(Continued)

Table 10.1 *(cont'd)*

What you want to do	How to do it	The result
Create the banner for the title.	<ul><li>Create a text box by selecting *Insert* on the toolbar, then choose *Text Box.*</li><li>Move the cursor to the spot on the poster where you want to place the banner.</li><li>Drag the mouse to indicate how wide the banner should be.</li><li>Put the cursor in the text box and select *Home* on the toolbar. Type the font size in the *Font* tab.</li><li>Depending on the length of the title, you might want to use a font of up to 72 point size. Type the title.</li><li>In the toolbar indicating font size, type the font size for authors' names and institutional affiliations (usually your school). You might use 48-point font for this.</li></ul>	This will let you type text to display wherever you want on the poster.

Table 10.2 Steps for Creating a PowerPoint® Poster Either on a Single, Large Sheet or on Multiple Sheets

What you want to do	How to do it	The result
Format a text box to enter material for your poster. (It is efficient to create a number of relatively small text boxes for individual elements of your poster.)	• Create a text box, select the font size you want to use (something around 40-point font), and type the text in it.	This will create a text box that is ready for typing.
	• Left-click in the text box to created the dotted border.	You will have to specify the size of the font you want each time you create a text box
	• Right-click and select *Format AutoShape*. • If you want the box to be a certain color, select your color in the box labeled *Fill*. • If you want a border around the box, select the color black (a neutral color) in the box for *Line → Color*. Under *Line → Style*, you can select line thickness.	
Import graphs from Excel® into your poster.	• In Excel®, create your graph.	This will move your graph from Excel® exactly as it appears in Excel®.
	• Copy the graph by highlighting it and either pressing CTRL + C or selecting *Edit* from the toolbar, then highlighting *Copy*. • Paste the graph into the poster by using CTRL + V or by selecting *Edit* from the toolbar, then highlighting *Paste*.	

(Continued)

Table 10.2 (*cont'd*)

What you want to do	How to do it	The result
Create a graph within PowerPoint®.	Select *Insert* from the toolbar and choose *Chart*. Select the kind of chart you want. PowerPoint® will present a display for typing in the labels and the numbers for your graph.	This will let you create a figure without exiting from PowerPoint®.
Move a graph.	• Left-click your mouse with the cursor in the graph. A dotted border will surround the graph. • Hold the mouse key down and drag the graph to the desired location.	This will allow you to place the graph where you want it.
Resize a graph.	• Left-click your mouse while the cursor is over one of the open circles on the border of the graph. • While holding the mouse button, move the cursor until the graph is the size you would like.	This will let you size your graph to fit with the text and other materials surrounding it.

Table 10.2   *(cont'd)*

What you want to do	How to do it	The result
Edit a graph in PowerPoint®.	• Double click on the graph. The graph will be surrounded by a dotted border, indicating that editing is possible. • Move the cursor to the area you want to edit and right-click. • Follow the same steps that you would to edit the figure in Excel®.	These steps allow you to change the lines in a line graph or the bars in a histogram or bar chart. You can also edit the figure title and the labels for the X- and Y-axes. You cannot edit the category labels. Note: If you make a change, you can reverse it by selecting *Edit* on the toolbar and highlighting *Undo*. If you reverse the change, you can bring back the change by selecting *Edit* and highlighting *Redo*. You can also use the *Undo* arrow or the *Redo* arrow replace both with 'undo' arrow used in Word

(Continued)

Table 10.2   (*cont'd*)

What you want to do	How to do it	The result
Import a table from Word®.	• Highlight the table in Word®.	This will allow you to reproduce the table exactly as it appears in the Word® document.
	• Copy the table using either CTRL + C or select *Edit* on the toolbar at the top and highlight *Copy*.	Note: You can edit the table once it is in PowerPoint® if you want to. See the steps below.
	• Paste the table into PowerPoint® using either CTRL + V or select *Edit* on the toolbar and highlight *Paste*.	
Edit a table in PowerPoint®.	• Double click on the table. The table will be surrounded by a dotted border, indicating that editing is possible.	These steps let you change the material in a table simply by retyping it. You can insert new rows and columns into the table.
	• Move the cursor to the text you want to edit and type the information as you would in a Word® document.	Note: If you make a change, you can reverse it by selecting *Edit* on the toolbar and highlighting *Undo*. If you reverse the change, you can bring back the

Table 10.2 (*cont'd*)

What you want to do	How to do it	The result
		change by selecting *Edit* and highlighting *Redo*. You can also use the *Undo* arrow the *Redo* arrow
	• To add a row at the end of the table, move the cursor to the last cell on the final line and press the *Tab* key. • To add a row anywhere, move the cursor to the row below where you want to put the new row, right-click on the mouse, and select *Insert Rows*. • To add a column, simply move the cursor to the cell where you want to insert values and type them in.	

The steps outlined in Table 10.1 pertain to creating a PowerPoint® poster on a single, large-sheet poster. Table 10.2 gives you guidance on creating any poster, whether on a single sheet or on multiple sheets.

11

Giving Oral Presentations

The human mind is a wonderful thing—it starts working the minute you're born and never stops until you get up to speak in public.
Attributed variously to syndicated columnist
Roscoe Drummond, comedian George Jessel,
and Mark Twain

According to most studies, people's number one fear is public speaking. Number two is death. ... This means to the average person, if you go to a funeral, you're better off in the casket than doing the eulogy.
Jerry Seinfeld

As the quotations above suggest, if people did not have to speak in public, most wouldn't. Fortunately, there are ways to make it enjoyable. The key is knowing what you want to say and preparing so that your time in front of the audience is more like engaging in a conversation and less like confronting a hostile group. Learning how to prepare and deliver a presentation is a skill that you can develop.

The Difference Between Oral and Written English

Imagine that you are listening to a group of researchers describing their research. Here is what they say:

APA Style Simplified: Writing in Psychology, Education, Nursing, and Sociology,
First Edition. Bernard C. Beins.
© 2012 John Wiley & Sons, Inc. Published 2012 by John Wiley & Sons, Inc.

As psychologists, we know a lot about empathy. We also know that people who are aggressive and antisocial show low levels of empathy, and they have a hard time putting themselves in the place of people around them. Unfortunately, we have a long way to go in understanding the lack of empathy in people with conduct disorders.

Now imagine that the same researchers said the following:

Deficiencies in empathy, defined as understanding and sharing in another's emotional state or context (Eisenberg & Strayer, 1987), have long been considered characteristic of aggressive and antisocial individuals (Cleckly, 1964; Hare, 1978; Hoffman, 1987). Although evidence also suggests that empathy facilitates prosocial behavior and reduces aggressive behavior in both children (Bryant, 1982; Eisenberg & Miller, 1987; Eisenberg-Berg & Lennon, 1980; Feshback, 1979; Feshback & Feshbach, 1982; Miller & Eisenberg, 1988; Poole, 1992) and adults (Batson, Fultz, & Schoenrade, 1987; Davis, Hull, Young, & Warren, 1987; Mehrabian & Epstein, 1972), few studies of empathy have been conducted directly with individuals demonstrating established histories of antisocial and aggressive conduct. Nor has research on antisocial youth kept pace with important refinements in both the operationalization of empathy and related developmental theory.

Which of the two would you rather listen to? Both passages present the same basic ideas. The first is simple and easy to understand. The second would be nearly incomprehensible as part of an oral presentation, although it would be fine as an opening paragraph in a published research report, which is what it is (Cohen & Strayer, 1996, p. 988).

These two passages demonstrate how you need to adapt your language to the type of presentation you make. If you are writing a paper, you can include a lot of background detail, many references, and technical language. But in an oral presentation, you need to keep your message simple. Keep your sentences short and to the point so that you can talk without getting stuck in the middle of a sentence and getting your audience stuck with you.

You are juggling two competing tendencies. If you include everything you know about the topic, you will present more information than a listener can possibly process. At the same time, if you don't offer important details, the listener will not be able to figure out why you did your research, how you did it, what you discovered, and what it means. Consequently, you have to decide which ideas are worth presenting and which ones you can omit and still get your message across. Table 11.1 highlights a strategy for preparing and organizing your talk.

Table 11.1 Guidelines for Presentation Material

Introduction	• Create an interesting and memorable opening that captures the audience's interest and focuses them on the two or three main points of your research; it can help the audience if you give a general sense of the important ideas and results that you are going to be presenting.
	• After you capture the audience's interest, identify and describe previous research findings that led to or relates to your research.
	• Don't bother identifying individual researchers unless they are particularly important and well known to the audience or unless they are critical to your audience's understanding.
	• State your hypotheses and tell how they connect to the research you have already described.
	• Restate and briefly summarize the logic that led you to your hypotheses from the prior research.
	• Throughout the presentation, create graphics to outline your main points. Keep the number of words on each slide to a minimum and use the graphics only to highlight your points. Don't make the audience read; get them to listen to you.
	• If you use a laser pointer to highlight material on slides, do so sparingly. Some people do not react well to a point of light bouncing across a screen.
Method	• *Participants*: Give the smallest amount of information that captures the nature of your participants adequately for understanding your research. Characterization of gender and ages may suffice unless you are investigating participant characteristics like ethnicity or background.
	• *Materials*: Identify the materials in enough detail for your audience to understand what the participants were exposed to.
	• Don't present as much detail as in a written paper, but make sure your audience understands your materials.
	• It can be helpful to create graphics to outline the nature of your materials.
	• *Procedure*: Outline what the participants did, giving enough detail to enable your audience to understand what the participants experienced.
	• It can be helpful to create graphics to demonstrate to the audience what the participants went through.

Table 11.1 *(cont'd)*

Results	• Rely on everyday English and simple descriptive statistics to describe the results, but have your inferential statistics handy in case people want details; a simple statement that the effects were significant will often suffice to give the audience a sense of the inferential statistics.
	• Tell whether the data supported your hypotheses.
	• Use graphics to present the technical aspects of statistical results so the audience can attend to them. You can rely on statements in everyday English to alert the audience to significant and nonsignificant results.
	• Create simple tables and figures to highlight results. If a graph or table is too cluttered or complex, the audience may not be able to pick out the important elements.
	• If you have multiple results to present, create separate figures and tables for each one.
	• If you have included material on a graph, draw it to the audience's attention. Otherwise, they may not know what you are referring to.
	• If you present numbers, figures, or tables on a slide, mention them and tell the audience what they signify. You know more about your topic than they do; give them the benefit of your knowledge by describing in words what the numbers and figures indicate. It may be helpful to use a pointer to let the audience know what part of your graph or table you are discussing.
Discussion	• Repeat your results only to highlight them and to refresh your audience's memory; describe the results briefly in everyday English and explain what those results tell you.
	• Connect the results to your hypotheses, saying whether the results supported your hypotheses.
	• Discuss why you think you obtained the results you did.
	• Finish with a strong summary that encapsulates what your results mean.
Question-and-answer period	• Don't be afraid to say you don't know the answer to a question.
	• If you know part of the answer to a question, tell what you know and say that you don't know the rest.
	• Don't hesitate to ask the questioner to explain a question if you don't understand it. If the person restates the question, it might give you additional cues about an appropriate response.

(Continued)

Table 11.1　*(cont'd)*

	• When somebody from the audience asks a question, repeat the question for the rest of the group. This guarantees that everybody can hear the question, and it gives you time to start thinking of an answer. • Pause and think about the question before you begin to answer it. A few moments of silence may feel very long to you, but the audience will not mind waiting for your response. • Ask the questioner if your response addressed the issue. It is appropriate to let the person offer his or her thoughts. You can gently ask, "Why might this be important?" • If a person in the audience tries to dominate the question-and-answer period, you can offer to talk to the person individually after the session. It is rude for a person to try to take over the question-and-answer period, so you are doing your audience a favor in letting others participate.
After the presentation	• Thank the audience for their attention. • Gather all of your materials, including any CDs, flash drives, the remote control for PowerPoint˚ presentation, or laser pointers that you brought with you. • Be prepared for an emotional letdown after you present. You will be stimulated before and during the talk. After you finish, it may take a little time to begin feeling normal again.

With a manuscript, a reader can go back and review earlier ideas. In an oral presentation, the listener has to keep everything you say in memory. As a result, you have to lead your listener on a well-planned path, making connections between ideas logical and apparent.

Adapting APA Style to Oral Presentations

As with poster presentations, in an oral presentation, you can modify your organization to fit your needs. Presenters typically follow the same general structure as they would in writing an APA-style paper, starting with an introduction, describing the methodology, then presenting the results, and concluding with a discussion. Unlike a paper, a presentation needs no abstract.

One of the important decisions to make about a presentation concerns references you might cite. As you can see in the Cohen and Strayer's (1996) passage at the beginning of this chapter, there are numerous references in the opening sentence of their paper. Just about all of them could be left out of an oral presentation. One reason is that none of them is absolutely vital for understanding where the research idea came from. Another reason is that, much of the time, people in the audience will not have heard of any of the researchers. Mentioning researchers unknown to the audience does not do anything to help them understand your point. So it doesn't pay to mention these authors.

There are exceptions to this last point. If you are presenting information to a group of experts in the area, they will be familiar with the research you cite, and they will expect you to discuss more technical detail. As such, it would be appropriate to mention by name the researchers whose ideas paved the way for your work. In addition, if your presentation involves describing a series of your own studies on a topic, your audience could benefit from knowing about the sequence of studies. In the end, you need to know your audience; if they are knowledgeable about your topic, they will be able to understand more complex ideas; if the audience consists of nonspecialists, you are better off omitting many of the technical details.

Preparing for Your Talk

The first step in organizing your talk is to determine what you want to tell your audience. Identify the two or three main ideas that you want the listeners to get. Then decide what information you need to present to achieve your goal. This process will result in decisions to omit a lot of information that you know. Some key steps in creating your presentation are given in Table 11.2.

As you prepare your talk, allocate specific amounts of time for each segment. If your presentation is 15 min, you could create a breakdown like this:

- Introduction—2 min
- Method—3 min
- Results—4 min
- Discussion—3 min
- Question and answer—3 min

Table 11.2   Creating Your Presentation

How to prepare	*Why you do it*
Identify three or four main points.	• Don't overload the listener with too much detail, but give the listener a sense of where your ideas are heading.
Decide how to introduce and explain the background and methodology related to your main points.	• Keep your presentation focused on the few key points you are addressing. • Get a feel for what ideas need to be repeated at various points during your talk.
Practice out loud.	• Give yourself a feel for what your presentation sounds like and how long it takes. • Work out a system in which a friend indicates to you if you are speaking too fast.
Set up a system like the one you will be using during your talk.	• Get comfortable with the technology so you can concentrate on the content of your presentation rather than on the equipment.
Prepare a backup.	• Sometimes technology fails. A handout (or transparencies if you know there will be an overhead projector) can provide a backup for getting your information across.

As you can see, you don't have a lot of time for any segment of your presentation. You will not be permitted to exceed your allotted time, so creating a coherent structure for your presentation is a good idea. In any case, if there are multiple presenters in your session, it would be rude to take time allotted to the other speakers. I once attended a session with three presenters. The first speaker took his allotted 15 min, but the second speaker talked for half an hour, leaving the final speaker about 5 min. The final speaker was very frustrated and the audience was irritated because they missed out on the ideas of that presenter. The middle speaker had clearly not prepared his talk in advance because he would have known that it was too lengthy.

After determining the two or three key points that listeners should remember, figure out the background that listeners should know if they are to follow your argument. Then include only the major points that led up to your work. Next, describe your methodology. Judicious use of a PowerPoint®

presentation (or transparencies for an overhead projector, although this equipment is getting somewhat rare) can help you present key elements of your method. Likewise, photographs of your apparatus may reduce the amount of time you need to spend on it.

Similarly, you should scale down the results, presenting only the most important and salient details. If you compare two groups and the difference is significant, you might display t-test results on a screen, but you don't need to mention it when you talk. It is sufficient to note that the difference is significant and which group has the higher mean. You can always fill in the details if somebody asks you a question about them. Finally, you will present your conclusions. It is a good idea to remind the audience of the logic of your research and how your results led to your ultimate conclusion. You might start your remarks here by identifying the main points that you will be discussing. This strategy will give the audience a refresher on your ideas and help them organize their own thoughts.

People can keep a few ideas in working memory, but if you tell them too much, they will lose the detail. So if they are not familiar with the nature of your research, you should show them only the tip of the iceberg. They won't be able to handle all the information that you want to give them. In general, they won't know you are leaving out a lot, and they won't care. If listeners do care about missing information, they can ask you a question, and you can respond.

When you organize your talk, figure out how to communicate with as little technical terminology as possible. It can help to work with a friend who can alert you when you are getting too complex. Sometimes you will have to convey technical information; that is fine, but if you overdo it, you may lose the audience.

Once you have organized the talk, prepare notes, then practice it out loud again and again so that you know what you want to say and how you are going to say it, and so that you have to refer to your notes as little as possible. It isn't possible to be overprepared. Rather, the more you practice your talk, the better your presentation will be.

Creating Graphics for Your Presentation

Presentation graphics have evolved from etched glass slides to photographic slides to overhead transparencies to PowerPoint® presentations. The flexibility of PowerPoint® is such that you can create just about any type of graphic that you desire. Ironically, even though you can generate a slide of any complexity you want, it is probably better to keep your slides simple.

The more information you try to convey on a slide, the harder it is for the audience to key in on the most important information. So keep your visual elements simple and to the point. In addition, in a professional talk, it is wise not to include sounds to introduce a new PowerPoint® slide. After a few slides, the sounds become distracting, then annoying (Daniel, 2004). It helps to refer to the material on your slides specifically. The audience does not always know what is the most critical information to focus on, so tell them where to look on the slide. This is easy to do with a laser pointer, but if you do not have one, you should still tell them where to look.

Giving the Presentation

There are a lot of details associated with a successful presentation. A high level of preparation is one of them (see Table 11.3 for guidance).

Your talk is a professional event. This means that you should act like a professional. The audience is expecting you to know something they don't, and they are there to gain from your expertise. In addition, they want you to succeed because if you don't succeed, they will be almost as unhappy as you. They will have to sit through a boring or incoherent presentation.

You are likely to be anxious about your talk. Recognizing that fact can help you deal with it; you are not alone—most speakers get nervous. There are ways to deal with the anxiety. To begin with, make sure you breathe normally. When people are nervous, they sometimes take gulps of air, talk until the air runs out, then they take another gulp. If you find yourself doing this, finish your sentence, take a deep breath, and pause a moment. It may also help to have water handy. Taking a drink can help you to relax.

Remember that the audience is interested in listening to you. Some basic tips can help keep their attention focused on you:

- Don't read from your notes; speak naturally, slowly, and with a relaxed voice. You may feel as if you are speaking at a normal conversational rate, but be aware that when you are nervous, there may be a tendency to speed up your rate of speech.
- Don't do PowerPoint® karaoke; that is, don't simply read from the screen. Use the slides only to offer highlights.

- Don't turn your back on the audience; face them and talk to them.
- Don't move around; stand still with your notes in front of you.

When you are giving your presentation, you may stumble across some of your words. We all do this at times. So if you begin talking and you lose your place, or if you have trouble pronouncing some words, stop and take a breath. If you need to go back to the beginning of your sentence, that is fine. Just do it smoothly. If you need to re-pronounce a word, just do that smoothly, too.

Table 11.3 Preparations at the Conference

What to do at the conference	Why you do it
Visit the presentation room.	• You can get a sense of what the room looks like, where people will be sitting, and what you need to do to be heard. • You can also see how to stand so you don't block the screen. • Arrange for a friend to sit within your line of sight. Your friend can signal if you are speaking too quickly.
Test the equipment.	• Sometimes the system you use for practice does not function like the system in the room. You don't want surprises when you plan for your presentation. • See what you have to do to get your presentation onto the system in the presentation room and what you need to do to access it right before your talk. • Make sure your PowerPoint® file is compatible with the equipment at the conference. For instance, sometimes graphics or videos do not transfer well from Macintosh computers to PCs. It would be a good idea to test this before you go to the conference, so that you can resolve any issues in advance.
Check your attire.	• If you have new clothes, make sure tags are removed. • Straighten anything that is unprofessional looking. • Some conferences provide doughnuts for attendees. It is probably not a good idea to eat powdered doughnuts if you are wearing a dark outfit.

You may be very aware of these slips in speech, but your audience will not be paying much attention to them. Professional speakers know that listeners don't really focus on interruptions in speech unless the speaker points them out. So don't point them out.

If you pay attention to other speakers, you will notice that, although their deliveries may be polished, they are not flawless. But most of the time, you won't even notice. During your presentation, your listeners will generally not be aware of small errors in your talk.

After you have completed your prepared remarks, expect some questions from the audience. Keep in mind that even experts don't know everything about their topic. As a speaker, you won't be expected to know everything, either. So if you forget something or if you can't answer a question, that's not necessarily a problem. You should prepare so that you minimize the need to say you don't know, but it will happen on occasion.

You are likely to be anxious before your presentation. That is completely natural. The better prepared you are, however, the less your anxiety will matter. You can harness your arousal to enhance your presentation. It might help you relax if you make eye contact with people in your audience, particularly friends who are there. Then, during your presentation, imagine you are talking to a friend.

12

Sharing Your Work Electronically

The new information technology, Internet and e-mail, have practically eliminated the physical costs of communications.

Peter Drucker

The Internet is clearly about more than sports scores and email now. It's a place where we can conduct our democracy and get very large amounts of data to very large numbers of people.

Frank James

The columnist Dave Barry seems to understand the Internet. He has said that "If you're willing to be patient, you'll find that you can utilize the vast resources of the Web to waste time in ways that you never before dreamed possible" (Barry, n.d.). Although people do spend a lot of time accessing Web sites, not all the time they spend on the Internet is wasted.

The Internet has emerged as a legitimate vehicle for disseminating information in the sciences. The number of Internet journals is increasing, and electronic books (e-books) have started appearing regularly. In addition, psychologists have begun posting their own writing to the Internet.

When psychologists publish their work on the Internet, it often undergoes peer review, in which experts have determined that the work is of high quality. Self-published work is of unknown quality, but you can find reliable information if you know where to look and how to evaluate Web sites.

APA Style Simplified: Writing in Psychology, Education, Nursing, and Sociology,
First Edition. Bernard C. Beins.
© 2012 John Wiley & Sons, Inc. Published 2012 by John Wiley & Sons, Inc.

Some people have taken word-processed documents and simply uploaded them to the Internet; others have converted their files to portable document format (the so-called *pdf* files). Manuscripts placed on the Internet through either of these approaches are likely to take the traditional APA-style format. But publishing in standard Internet format, using hypertext markup language (HTML), has some advantages that you don't see with either word-processed or pdf files.

New Capabilities in Electronic Sharing

Undoubtedly, the most important feature of Internet publishing is that it allows quick dissemination of your work to a world-wide audience. Another feature of Internet publishing involves the use of hyperlinks. Internet users take it for granted that they can click on a link and go to a site that offers information related to a topic. If you post your work to the Internet, you can send your reader to:

- another paper you have written;
- a Web site that will further explain the point you are making;
- an image or a figure you have created;
- a citation in your reference list.

When you use hyperlinks, you are making it a little easier for your reader to understand your ideas and the context in which you are presenting them. The downside, of course, is that the reader may face an inordinate amount of information, too much to process at more than a cursory level.

Other elements that you can include in your Internet presentation are audio and video files. So if you are conducting research that makes use of audio or video stimuli, you can save such files on your server and let your readers see or hear them while they are reading your manuscript. Traditionally, journals have been reluctant to publish pictures because images have to be processed and formatted individually, so they are expensive. The journals of the Association for Psychological Science will print one image in color without cost in a journal article, but authors must pay $250 (as of 2011) for each additional image in color. Furthermore, pictures take up a lot of journal space. A journal in print format can publish only a limited number of pages per issue or per volume, so space is at a premium.

Internet space is less expensive than paper space. So although publishing a large number of images on paper is not feasible, it is quite reasonable in electronic space. Publishing video and audio is impossible on paper, but very simple electronically.

Using a Word Processor to Create Manuscripts for the Internet

Creating a file for the Internet, an HTML file, is very easy. Table 12.1 shows the basic steps using Word®. You can create a basic Web page by writing your paper, then easily saving it in Web-compatible format.

If you create a manuscript for the Internet, you need to remember a couple of important details. First, the file name should not contain any spaces. In Word®, file names can have spaces, but Internet files cannot; names of Web pages must consist of an uninterrupted string of characters. (Your computer may fill in spaces with characters like percent signs, which will make the title less obvious.) When authors want to use multiple words in a file name, they typically separate words with a dash (e.g., *my-file*) or with an underscore (e.g., *my_file*).

A second detail to remember is that if you are likely to publish a number of documents on the Internet, you would do well to figure out a consistent way of naming your files so you can establish a pattern that is easy for you to remember—for example, using only lowercase letters in file names and separating words with a single dash. It doesn't really matter what convention you choose, but consistency makes life easier in remembering how you name files.

Table 12.1   Saving a Word® Manuscript in a Format for Internet Publishing

Word® version 1	*Word® version 2*
Click on *Word Office* icon from the menu at the top left of the page. Select Save As.	Click on *Save As* if it appears on the menu at the top of the page.
In the box labeled *Save as type*, select *Web Page*.	
Save the file with a title that has no spaces. Use a dash-like-this or an underscore_like_this if you want to create a title that has multiple words. Or you can just create a title with no break between wordslikethis.	

Creating Hyperlinks

If you create a manuscript with a word-processing program, it is easy to create hyperlinks in the text. The effect will be to allow the reader to click on a section of text and go either to a different Web site or to a different spot in the current document. Tables 12.2 and 12.3 illustrate how to insert hyperlinks for these uses. When is it helpful to create hyperlinks? Any time you think that your reader could benefit from additional information.

A common use of hyperlinks in online journals is for citing references. If you discuss previous research, you need to cite the article in your References section. Authors frequently create a hyperlink when they mention an article in the text so that when the reader clicks on the link, the Web browser goes to the appropriate citation in the reference list.

Table 12.2   Creating a Hyperlink to an Internet Location Outside Your Own Web Document

Word®
Highlight the word or words you want to hyperlink.

Select *Insert* → *Links* from the menu at the top of the page
OR
Type *CTRL K*.
In the box labeled *Address* type the URL (i.e., the Web address) of the document to which you want to link.
Select OK.

Note: You use the same series of steps for linking to any kind of file, including text, audio, and video files.

Table 12.3   Creating a Hyperlink to a Location Within Your Own Web Document Using Word®

Highlight the text where the hyperlink will take you in the document; this is the destination when a user clicks on the link.
Select *Insert* on the menu at the top of the page.
Click on *Bookmark* and type in a name for the bookmark.
The first word of the text that is hyperlinked can serve as a good name for the bookmark, but you can create any label you want.
Select *Insert* on the menu at the top of the page and click on *Hyperlink*, selecting "Place in this document."
Select *Bookmark* and choose the appropriate bookmark name.
Click *OK*.

Note: You can test to see if your bookmark works by holding the control key and clicking on the text that is the starting point.

Inserting Images

If you have pictures or graphs you want to insert into your manuscript, you can accomplish this easily. All you have to do is to display the image on your computer monitor, copy it, then paste it into the document where you want it. If you upload a word-processed document to the Internet, a reader will open it as with any word-processed file. It will look just as it did when you created it.

If you save a Web page document (i.e., a document in HTML format) with images, those images are saved separately from your original document. So you must upload not only the manuscript but also the images. If you don't save the images separately, you will be able to open a Word file saved in HTML format on your computer, and the images will be there. But if you upload your file to an Internet server, you will need to upload the picture files to a folder on the server.

If you have graphs that you want to insert, you can present a thumbnail— that is, a version that presents the graph in a size that gives a sense of the results but that is small enough to fit within the text. If you create a hyperlink from the thumbnail to the full-sized version, the reader can click on the small version to get the full-sized picture.

Advantages of Internet Publishing Software

Although the most convenient way to create an Internet manuscript may be by using the common word-processing programs, there are some advantages to using Internet publishing software programs such as FrontPage® or Dreamweaver®. These programs are easy to understand and use, and they offer features that make formatting quite easy.

With some practice, you should be able to put together a competent Internet manuscript with the Internet publishing software, but it will take a little time for you to learn about the special features of the programs. One of the advantages of this software is that you can include elements known as *metatags*. The most important of these tags is the title metatag, which tells your Web browser to insert a title at the very top of the display. Other types of tags can provide information about the author of the Web page, its title, its contents, and descriptors of its content.

The Internet publishing software is also useful because it provides more flexibility in formatting your work. Some of the features that are easy to

Table 12.4   Useful Features of Internet Publishing Software That Are Not as Easy or are Impossible with Word Processors

Feature	Why the feature is useful
Creating a title metatag	This tells your Web browser to put the title of your document at the top of the window containing your document.
Opening hyperlinks in separate pages	You can send the reader to a new Web site without closing the window with your work on it. This feature makes it easier for the reader to get back to your Web document.
Manipulating images	You can size images as you desire. In addition, you can wrap text around the images, putting the image on the left margin, for example, and putting text above it, to the side, and below.
Using background color and "wallpaper"	You can add color and patterns to the background of your Web page. It can make them more attractive and, perhaps, easier to read with the right color combinations.
Using tables to format your Web page	You can create tables that help you format your Web document and organize the content. You can hide the lines of the table. Many Web pages use tables in their layout.
Sizing fonts in your document	Word-processing programs let you size text easily, but with Internet publishing software, it is easier to make changes and to see their effect immediately.
Creating email links	You can easily create a hyperlink that lets a reader email you.

implement with this software appear in Table 12.4. They include such details as sizing and placement of tables, figures, and text. But there are many other useful features that you can learn as you develop your skills. You can also select background colors or wallpaper patterns to make your Web manuscript easier to read or to make it look more appealing. In word processing, these tasks are either difficult or impossible because the primary purpose of that software is not to create Internet documents.

If all you intend to do is to post your manuscript on the Internet, a word-processing program provides a very easy tool for doing so. Internet publishing software has an incredible array of features, and it allows you to generate some interesting and useful effects, but for putting a standard APA-format paper on the Web, word processing will work pretty well. And if you are writing the paper to begin with, it really doesn't take all that much extra work to publish it on the Internet with some of the helpful features such as hyperlinks.

Publishing Your Poster on the Web

If you create a single-sheet poster using PowerPoint®, you can also publish it on the Internet. All you need to do to save it in a format compatible with the Internet is to choose the *Save As* function, then save it using the file type *Single File Web Page*. Some browsers may not accept this type of file, so you should try it to see in what conditions it works.

Uploading Your Manuscript to the Internet

This chapter highlights the basics of creating a manuscript that you can publish on the Internet. Word processors are adequate for creating a basic Internet document. You can probably accomplish just about anything you need to in a research report. But there will be limitations regarding the flexibility of formatting provided by such software.

Regardless of how you create the manuscript, though, you need to get it onto a server that allows Internet users to access it. How to place your information on a server is beyond the scope of this book, but colleges and universities typically let students and faculty develop Web sites. Commercial organizations also sell space on servers.

Regardless of which approach you choose, software will be available to move your files from your computer to a server. After that, your work will be part of the Internet.

In addition to saving your work online as a Web page, you can back up your work and share it with others with services provided by organizations like Google with their Google Docs service or in backup sites like Dropbox. These are not the only sites that allow backup and sharing, but they are among the most common. With these (and others), you can save your files so they are accessible from any computer that has Internet access.

One advantage of sites like these is that you can identify people who can access the material. So if you are working on a group project, everybody in your group can get to the documents and revise them. This feature eliminates the need to send a document to one person at a time, with each person in the group revising the work before forwarding it to the next person.

Revisiting the Concept of Plagiarism

Over the past decade, psychologists have made their work freely available on the Internet. The amount of high-quality work is large, and it continues to increase. (Of course, the amount of questionable work is on the increase, too.) The nature of electronic publishing is such that it is possible to take work on the Internet and import it directly into one's own documents. This fact can be a source of problems.

There seems to be a general belief on the part of many that if something is easily available via the Internet, that material is in the public domain. That is, many people think that they can simply incorporate that material without any attribution and use it as if they owned it. Another complication is that authors of some of the material on the Internet expect payment if others use their work. Using work without attributing it to the author and using it without payment is unethical.

The doctrine of fair use allows a person to use copyrighted material in certain circumstances, as in education, but the policies associated with fair use are not entirely clear. So if you are going to take material from the Internet, you must cite the source. In addition, you cannot use it if your intended use goes beyond what the author stipulated is appropriate.

The issues of plagiarism are complicated by the ubiquity of material on the Internet and the ease with which you can expropriate it. It is important to write ethically, avoiding plagiarism and other copyright infringement.

Appendix A

Example of APA-Style Manuscript with Common Errors

When you write an APA-style paper, there are many details to remember. In this appendix, the sample manuscript illustrates the use of APA style and common errors that writers make.

APA Style Simplified: Writing in Psychology, Education, Nursing, and Sociology,
First Edition. Bernard C. Beins.
© 2012 John Wiley & Sons, Inc. Published 2012 by John Wiley & Sons, Inc.

Running head: IS THIS JOKE FUNNY?   1

Is This Joke Funny?: Only If We Say It Is

Wilhelm Wundt

Mann-Whitney U.

> Everything should be double spaced.

> APA—Write out *University* in its entirety.

> If an Author Note is required, position it here. However, student papers rarely require notes.

2   IS THIS JOKE FUNNY?

Abstract

    In two experiments, participants read and rated a set of jokes for their humor value. In each experiment, participants were told that the jokes had been rated previously. In different conditions, participants believed that the jokes had been rated low or rated high by others. The results showed that when participants thought the jokes had been rated as very funny, his/her own ratings tended to be high. When participants thought the jokes had been rated as not very funny, their own ratings were low. In a control condition where participants did not learn that others had rated the jokes, their ratings were between those of the other groups. I concluded that, because jokes do not have an intrinsic humor level, people rely on cues from others to help them decide how funny they are.

    Keywords: Humor, priming

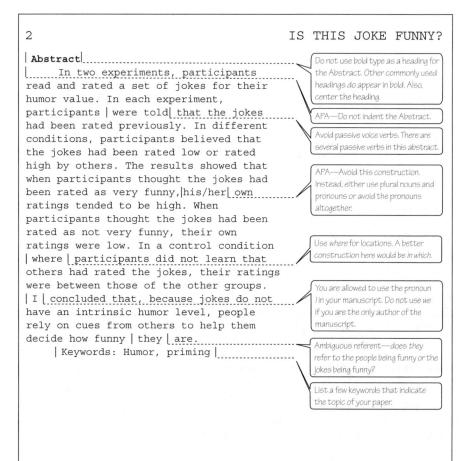

Do not use bold type as a heading for the Abstract. Other commonly used headings do appear in bold. Also, center the heading.

APA—Do not indent the Abstract.

Avoid passive voice verbs. There are several passive verbs in this abstract.

APA—Avoid this construction. Instead, either use plural nouns and pronouns or avoid the pronouns altogether.

Use *where* for locations. A better construction here would be *in which*.

You are allowed to use the pronoun *I* in your manuscript. Do not use *we* if you are the only author of the manuscript.

Ambiguous referent—does *they* refer to the people being funny or the jokes being funny?

List a few keywords that indicate the topic of your paper.

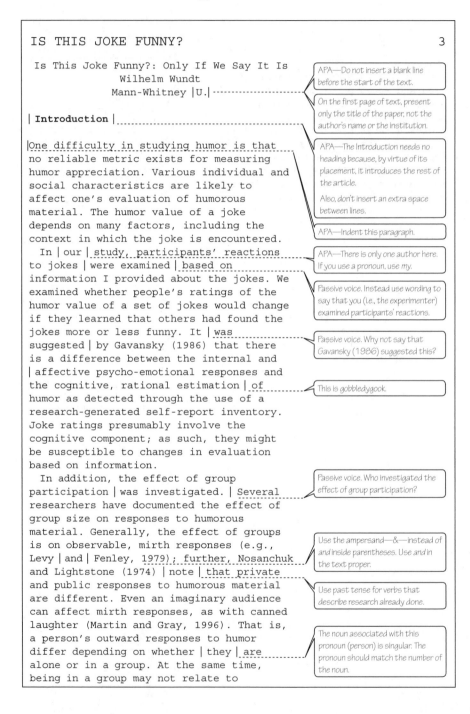

IS THIS JOKE FUNNY? 3

Is This Joke Funny?: Only If We Say It Is
Wilhelm Wundt
Mann-Whitney |U.|

> APA—Do not insert a blank line before the start of the text.

> On the first page of text, present only the title of the paper, not the author's name or the institution.

| Introduction |

> APA—The Introduction needs no heading because, by virtue of its placement, it introduces the rest of the article.
>
> Also, don't insert an extra space between lines.

|One difficulty in studying humor is that no reliable metric exists for measuring humor appreciation. Various individual and social characteristics are likely to affect one's evaluation of humorous material. The humor value of a joke depends on many factors, including the context in which the joke is encountered.

> APA—Indent this paragraph.

In | our | study, participants' reactions to jokes | were examined | based on information I provided about the jokes. We examined whether people's ratings of the humor value of a set of jokes would change if they learned that others had found the jokes more or less funny. It | was suggested | by Gavansky (1986) that there is a difference between the internal and | affective psycho-emotional responses and the cognitive, rational estimation | of humor as detected through the use of a research-generated self-report inventory. Joke ratings presumably involve the cognitive component; as such, they might be susceptible to changes in evaluation based on information.

> APA—There is only one author here. If you use a pronoun, use *my*.

> Passive voice. Instead use wording to say that you (i.e., the experimenter) examined participants' reactions.

> Passive voice. Why not say that Gavansky (1986) suggested this?

> This is gobbledygook.

In addition, the effect of group participation | was investigated. | Several researchers have documented the effect of group size on responses to humorous material. Generally, the effect of groups is on observable, mirth responses (e.g., Levy | and | Fenley, 1979); further, Nosanchuk and Lightstone (1974) | note | that private and public responses to humorous material are different. Even an imaginary audience can affect mirth responses, as with canned laughter (Martin and Gray, 1996). That is, a person's outward responses to humor differ depending on whether | they | are alone or in a group. At the same time, being in a group may not relate to

> Passive voice. Who investigated the effect of group participation?

> Use the ampersand—&—instead of *and* inside parentheses. Use *and* in the text proper.

> Use past tense for verbs that describe research already done.

> The noun associated with this pronoun (person) is singular. The pronoun should match the number of the noun.

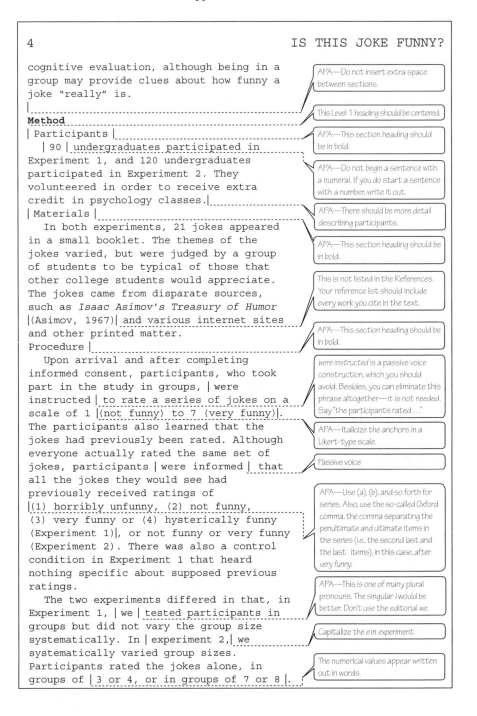

4   IS THIS JOKE FUNNY?

cognitive evaluation, although being in a group may provide clues about how funny a joke "really" is.

Method

Participants

90 undergraduates participated in Experiment 1, and 120 undergraduates participated in Experiment 2. They volunteered in order to receive extra credit in psychology classes.

Materials

In both experiments, 21 jokes appeared in a small booklet. The themes of the jokes varied, but were judged by a group of students to be typical of those that other college students would appreciate. The jokes came from disparate sources, such as *Isaac Asimov's Treasury of Humor* (Asimov, 1967) and various internet sites and other printed matter.

Procedure

Upon arrival and after completing informed consent, participants, who took part in the study in groups, were instructed to rate a series of jokes on a scale of 1 (not funny) to 7 (very funny). The participants also learned that the jokes had previously been rated. Although everyone actually rated the same set of jokes, participants were informed that all the jokes they would see had previously received ratings of (1) horribly unfunny, (2) not funny, (3) very funny or (4) hysterically funny (Experiment 1), or not funny or very funny (Experiment 2). There was also a control condition in Experiment 1 that heard nothing specific about supposed previous ratings.

The two experiments differed in that, in Experiment 1, we tested participants in groups but did not vary the group size systematically. In experiment 2, we systematically varied group sizes. Participants rated the jokes alone, in groups of 3 or 4, or in groups of 7 or 8.

Annotations:

APA—Do not insert extra space between sections.

This Level 1 heading should be centered.

APA—This section heading should be in bold.

APA—Do not begin a sentence with a numeral. If you do start a sentence with a number, write it out.

APA—There should be more detail describing participants.

APA—This section heading should be in bold.

This is not listed in the References. Your reference list should include every work you cite in the text.

APA—This section heading should be in bold.

were instructed is a passive voice construction, which you should avoid. Besides, you can eliminate this phrase altogether—it is not needed. Say "the participants rated..."

APA—Italicize the anchors in a Likert-type scale.

Passive voice

APA—Use (a), (b), and so forth for series. Also, use the so-called Oxford comma, the comma separating the penultimate and ultimate items in the series (i.e., the second last and the last items), in this case, after very funny.

APA—This is one of many plural pronouns. The singular I would be better. Don't use the editorial we.

Capitalize the e in experiment.

The numerical values appear written out in words.

IS THIS JOKE FUNNY? 5

Results and Discussion

In Experiment 1, after learning about previous ratings, the jokes were rated differently, $F=8.591$, $p=.000$. When participants did not have expectations about the jokes, they rated them in the middle.

While it is possible that participants were responding to demand characteristics, I do not believe this is true because the two extreme groups, Hysterically Funny and Horribly Unfunny, received the same ratings as the neutral group. Thus, our participants were quite capable of ignoring information that was clearly discrepant with reality. In fact, the jokes were neither horrible nor wonderful. The data shows that the ratings in the neutral group fell slightly more positively than the middle point on a 7-point scale. When being debriefed, the manipulation wasn't obvious to the participants.

In Experiment 2, I eliminated the two extreme categories (Hysterically Funny and Horribly Unfunny) and repeated the study with a systematic examination of the effects of group size. Previous research has suggested that being part of a group affects humor responses. If rating the jokes involves a cognitive evaluation, however, we might not expect to see an effect of group size on ratings, although outward expression of mirth might be susceptible to group effects (for example, Levy and Fenley, 1979).

The second study produced the same effect of information on putative funniness of the jokes, $F=9.878$, $p=.000$. Jokes that were supposed to be funny were rated as such; jokes that were not supposed to be funny were not. Table 1 presents these results.

There wasn't an effect of group size on joke ratings, $F=0.426$, $p=.654$. There was also no interaction between

---

Margin annotations:

- This Level 1 heading should be centered.
- In a paper with a single study, it can be appropriate to combine the Results and the Discussion sections. In longer papers, you use separate sections for the two.
- Passive voice
- Misplaced modifier: the jokes did not learn about previous ratings; the participants did.
- Throughout the results, statistical tests and p-values should be italicized. APA—You need to indicate degrees of freedom. In addition, when the probability value is .000 when you carry it to three decimal places, use $p < .001$.
- *While* is a conjunction involving time. Do not use it when you mean *although* or *whereas*.
- APA—Group names should appear in lower case.
- *Data* is plural, so this should be *data show*.
- This is a misplaced modifier—the manipulation was not debriefed, the participants were.
- Avoid contractions in formal writing.
- Avoid the editorial *we*.
- Use Latin—*et al.*—within parentheses. Use English—*for example*—outside of parentheses.
- APA—**Within parentheses**, use an ampersand (&) in the list of authors. If the authors are mentioned **outside** of parentheses, use the word *and*.
- APA—Degrees of freedom?
- Use $p < .001$ in APA style. In any case, it would be inappropriate to say $p = 0$ (with no decimal places).
- Avoid contractions in formal writing.
- APA—Degrees of freedom? Also, use italics for the statistic and the probability value.

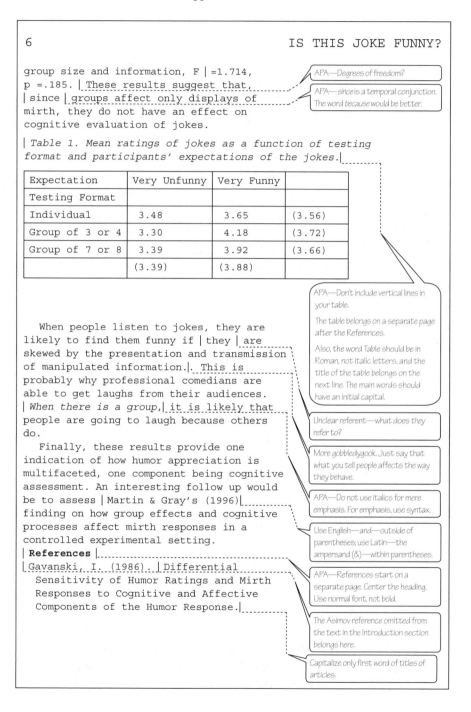

6   IS THIS JOKE FUNNY?

group size and information, F | =1.714, p =.185. | These results suggest that, | since | groups affect only displays of mirth, they do not have an effect on cognitive evaluation of jokes.

APA—Degrees of freedom?

APA—since is a temporal conjunction. The word because would be better.

| Table 1. Mean ratings of jokes as a function of testing format and participants' expectations of the jokes.|

Expectation / Testing Format	Very Unfunny	Very Funny	
Individual	3.48	3.65	(3.56)
Group of 3 or 4	3.30	4.18	(3.72)
Group of 7 or 8	3.39	3.92	(3.66)
	(3.39)	(3.88)	

APA—Don't include vertical lines in your table.

The table belongs on a separate page after the References.

Also, the word Table should be in Roman, not italic letters, and the title of the table belongs on the next line. The main words should have an initial capital.

When people listen to jokes, they are likely to find them funny if | they | are skewed by the presentation and transmission of manipulated information.|. This is probably why professional comedians are able to get laughs from their audiences. | When there is a group,| it is likely that people are going to laugh because others do.

Finally, these results provide one indication of how humor appreciation is multifaceted, one component being cognitive assessment. An interesting follow up would be to assess | Martin & Gray's (1996)| finding on how group effects and cognitive processes affect mirth responses in a controlled experimental setting.

Unclear referent—what does they refer to?

More gobbledygook. Just say that what you tell people affects the way they behave.

APA—Do not use italics for mere emphasis. For emphasis, use syntax.

Use English—and—outside of parentheses; use Latin—the ampersand (&)—within parentheses.

| **References** |

| Gavanski, I. (1986). | Differential Sensitivity of Humor Ratings and Mirth Responses to Cognitive and Affective Components of the Humor Response.|

APA—References start on a separate page. Center the heading. Use normal font, not bold.

The Asimov reference omitted from the text in the Introduction section belongs here.

Capitalize only first word of titles of articles.

IS THIS JOKE FUNNY? 7

Journal of Personality and Social Psychology, |51(1)|, 209-2|14| .

> Include the issue number only if pagination in every issue starts at page 1.

Levy, S. G., & Fenley, W. F. (1979). Audience Size and Likelihood and Intensity of Response During a Humorous Movie. *Bulletin of the Psychonomic Society, 13(6)*, 409-412.

> APA—Put the *doi* after the reference. For the Gavanski citation, the *doi* information would look like this:
> *doi*:10.1037/0022-3514.51.1.209
>
> Not all journal articles have a *doi*. For example, the Levy & Fenley article does not. Most journal articles do have such an indicator.

Martin, G. N., & Gray, C. D. (1996). The Effects of Audience Laughter on Men's and Women's Responses to Humor. | The | *Journal of Social Psychology, 136(2)*, 221-231.

Nosanchuk, T. A., & Lightstone, J. (1974). Canned Laughter and Public and Private Conformity. *Journal of Personality and Social Psychology, 29(1)*, 153-156.

> APA—No need to include the definite article in journal titles.

Appendix B

Corrected APA-Style Manuscript

The manuscript in this appendix shows how you create and format a manuscript in correct APA style. I have corrected the errors in the previous appendix, so the version here conforms to APA guidelines. This example includes two experiments. In most papers, you would include separate sections for the two studies, but for the purposes of this example, I have combined them so the manuscript has the format you would use for a paper that reports a single study. Manuscripts should be double spaced. This sample is not double spaced in order to save space in this book.

APA Style Simplified: Writing in Psychology, Education, Nursing, and Sociology,
First Edition. Bernard C. Beins.
© 2012 John Wiley & Sons, Inc. Published 2012 by John Wiley & Sons, Inc.

Running head: IS THIS JOKE FUNNY?   1

Is This Joke Funny?: Only If We Say It Is

Wilhelm Wundt

Mann-Whitney University

Abstract

In two experiments, participants read and rated a set of jokes for their humor value. In each experiment, participants heard that the jokes had been rated previously. In different conditions, participants believed that the jokes had been rated low or rated high by others. The results showed that when participants thought the jokes had been rated as very funny, their own ratings tended to be high. When participants thought that others had rated the jokes as not very funny, their own ratings were low. In a control condition in which participants did not learn that others had rated the jokes, their ratings were between those of the other groups. The results suggest that, because jokes do not have an intrinsic humor level, people rely on cues from others to help them decide how funny the jokes are.

Keywords: believability, group size, humor appreciation, joke ratings, persuasion

Is This Joke Funny? Only If We Say It Is

One difficulty in studying humor is that no reliable metric exists for measuring humor appreciation. Various individual and social characteristics are likely to affect one's evaluation of humorous material. The humor value of a joke depends on many factors, including the context in which the joke is encountered.

In the present study, I examined participants' reactions to jokes based on information I provided about the jokes. The research examined whether people's ratings of the humor value of a set of jokes would change if they learned that others had found the jokes more or less funny. Gavansky (1986) suggested that there is a difference between the internal and affective, emotional responses and the cognitive ratings of humor. Because joke ratings presumably involve the cognitive component, they might be susceptible to changes in evaluation based on information.

In addition, the research focused on the effect of group participation. Several researchers have documented the effect of group size on responses to humorous material. Generally, the effect of groups is on observable, mirth responses (e.g., Levy & Fenley, 1979); further, Nosanchuk and Lightstone (1974) noted that private and public responses to humorous material are different. Even an imaginary audience can affect mirth responses, as with canned laughter (Martin & Gray, 1996). That is, people's outward responses to humor differ depending on whether they are alone or in a group. At the same time, being in a group may not relate to cognitive evaluation, although being in a group may provide clues about how funny a joke "really" is.

Method
Participants
Ninety undergraduates participated in Experiment 1, and 120 undergraduates participated in Experiment 2. They volunteered in order to receive extra credit in psychology classes. The participants in the first study included 61 women and 29 men whose ages ranged from 17 to 23 years ($M = 18.9$, $SD = 1.2$). The sample in the second study consisted of 83 women and 37 men whose ages ranged from 18 to 23 ($M = 19.1$, $SD = 1.1$). They volunteered in order to receive extra credit in psychology classes.

Materials
In both experiments, 21 jokes appeared in a small booklet. The themes of the jokes varied, but were judged by a group of students to be typical of those that other college students would appreciate. The jokes came from disparate sources, such as *Isaac Asimov's Treasury of Humor* (Asimov, 1967) and various Internet sites and other printed matter.

Procedure
Upon arrival and after completing informed consent, participants, who took part in the study in groups, rated a series of jokes on a scale of 1 (*not funny*) to 7 (*very funny*). The participants also learned that the jokes had previously been rated. Although everyone actually rated the same set of jokes, participants learned from the experimenter that all the jokes they would see had previously received ratings of (a) horribly

unfunny, (b) not funny, (c) very funny, or (d) hysterically funny (Experiment 1), or not funny or very funny (Experiment 2). There was also a control condition in Experiment 1 that heard nothing specific about supposed previous ratings.

The two experiments differed in that, in Experiment 1, participants were in groups but I did not vary the group size systematically. In Experiment 2, I systematically varied group sizes. Participants rated the jokes alone, in groups of three or four, or in groups of seven or eight.

Results and Discussion

In Experiment 1, after learning about previous ratings, participants rated the jokes differently, $F(4, 85) = 8.591$, $p < .001$. When participants did not have expectations about the jokes, they rated them in the middle.

Although it is possible that participants were responding to demand characteristics, I do not believe this is true because the two extreme groups, hysterically funny and horribly unfunny, received the same ratings as the neutral group. Thus, our participants were quite capable of ignoring information that was clearly discrepant with reality. In fact, the jokes were neither horrible nor wonderful. The data show that the ratings in the neutral group fell slightly more positively than the middle point on a 7-point scale. When being debriefed, the participants reported that manipulation was not obvious to them.

In Experiment 2, I eliminated the two extreme categories (hysterically funny and horribly unfunny) and repeated the study with a systematic

6   IS THIS JOKE FUNNY?

examination of the effects of group size. Previous research has suggested that being part of a group affects humor responses. If rating the jokes involves a cognitive evaluation, however, one might not expect to see an effect of group size on ratings, although outward expression of mirth might be susceptible to group effects (e.g., Levy & Fenley, 1979).

The second study produced the same effect of information on putative funniness of the jokes, $F(2, 114) = 9.878$, $p < .001$. Participants rated jokes that were supposed to be funny as such; jokes that were not supposed to be funny received lower ratings. Table 1 presents these results. There was no effect of group size on joke ratings, $F(2, 114) = 0.426$, $p = .654$. There was also no interaction between group size and information, $F(2, 114) = 1.714$, $p = .185$. These results suggest that, because group size affects only displays of mirth, they do not have an effect on cognitive evaluation of jokes.

People listening to jokes are likely to find the jokes funny if they receive information that predisposes them to view the humor as funny. This phenomenon is probably why professional comedians are able to get laughs from their audiences. When there is a group, it is likely that people are going to laugh because others do.

Finally, these results provide one indication of how humor appreciation is multifaceted, one component being cognitive assessment. An interesting follow up would be to assess Martin and Gray's (1996) finding on how group effects and cognitive processes affect affective, mirth responses in a controlled experimental setting.

References

Asimov, I. (1967). *Isaac Asimov's treasury of humor*. Boston, MA: Houghton Mifflin.

Gavanski, I. (1986). Differential sensitivity of humor ratings and mirth responses to cognitive and affective components of the humor response. *Journal of Personality and Social Psychology, 51*, 209–214. doi:10.1037/0022-3514.51.1.209

Levy, S. G., & Fenley, W. F. (1979). Audience size and likelihood and intensity of response during a humorous movie. *Bulletin of the Psychonomic Society, 13*, 409–412.

Martin, G. N., & Gray, C. D. (1996). The effects of audience laughter on men's and women's responses to humor. *Journal of Social Psychology, 136*, 221–231. doi:10.1016/S0031-9384(96)80017-5

Nosanchuk, T. A., & Lightstone, J. (1974). Canned laughter and public and private conformity. *Journal of Personality and Social Psychology, 29*, 153–156. doi:10.1037/h0035737

8   IS THIS JOKE FUNNY?

Table 1.
Mean Ratings of Jokes as a Function of Testing Format and Participants' Expectations of the Jokes

	Expectation		
	Very Unfunny	Very Funny	
Testing Format			
Individual	3.48	3.65	(3.56)
Group of 3 or 4	3.30	4.18	(3.72)
Group of 7 or 8	3.39	3.92	(3.66)
	(3.39)	(3.88)	

References

Abu-Bader, S. H., Tirmazi, M., & Ross-Sheriff, F. (2011). The impact of acculturation on depression among older Muslim immigrants in the United States. *Journal of Gerontological Social Work, 54*, 425–448. doi:10.1080/01634372.2011.560928

AbuSeileek, A. F. (2011). Hypermedia annotation presentation: The effect of location and type on the ELF learners' achievement in reading comprehension and vocabulary acquisition. *Computers & Education, 57*, 1281–1291. doi:10.1016/j.compedu.2011.01.011

Adams, D. M., Mayer, R. E., MacNamara, A., Koenig, A., & Wainess, R. (2011, September 26). Narrative games for learning: Testing the discovery and narrative hypotheses. *Journal of Educational Psychology*. Advance online publication. doi: 10.1037/a0025595

American Psychological Association (2001). *Publication manual of the American Psychological Association* (5th ed.). Washington, DC: Author.

American Psychological Association (Ed.). (2007). *Getting in: A step-by-step plan for gaining admission to graduate school in psychology* (2nd ed.). Washington, DC: Author.

American Psychological Association (2010). *Publication manual of the American Psychological Association* (6th ed.). Washington, DC: Author.

Barry, D. (n.d.). The internet explained. Retrieved January 29, 2007 from http://www.geocities.com/CollegePark/6174/db-internet.htm

Becker, E. (1973). *The denial of death*. New York: Free Press.

Beins, B. C. (1993). Writing assignments in statistics classes encourage students to learn interpretation. *Teaching of Psychology, 20*, 161–164.

Beins, B. C. (2006). The scholarship of teaching and pedagogy. In W. Buskist and S. F. Davis (Eds.), *Handbook of the teaching of psychology* (pp. 11–15). Malden, MA: Blackwell.

APA Style Simplified: Writing in Psychology, Education, Nursing, and Sociology, First Edition. Bernard C. Beins.
© 2012 John Wiley & Sons, Inc. Published 2012 by John Wiley & Sons, Inc.

Beins, B. C. (2009). *Research methods: A tool for life* (2nd ed.). Boston, MA: Allyn & Bacon.

Beins, B. C., Agnitti, J., Baldwin, V., Lapham, H., Yarmosky, S., Bubel, A., MacNaughton, K., & Pashka, N. (2005, October). How expectations affect perceptions of offensive humor. Poster presented at the annual convention of the New England Psychological Association, New Haven, CT.

Beran, M. J., Smith, J. D., Redford, J. S., & Washburn, D. A. (2006). Rhesus macaques (*Macaca mulatta*) monitor uncertainty during numerosity judgments. *Journal of Experimental Psychology: Animal Behavior Processes, 32,* 111–119.

Best, J. (2001). *Damned lies and statistics: Untangling numbers from the media, politicians, and activists.* Berkeley: University of California Press.

Best, J. (2004). *More damned lies and statistics: How numbers confuse public issues.* Berkeley: University of California Press.

Boag, S. (2006). Freudian repression, the common view, and pathological science. *Review of General Psychology, 10,* 74–86. doi:10.1037/1089-2680.10.1.74

Braveman, P. A., Kumanyika, S., Fielding, J., LaVeist, T., Borrell, L. N., Manderscheid, R., & Troutman, A. (2011). Health disparities and health equity: The issue is justice. *American Journal of Public Health, 101,* S149–S155. doi:10.2105/AJPH.2010.300062

Brewer, B. W., Scherzer, C. B., Van Raaltel, J. L., Petitpas, A. J., & Andersen, M. B. (2001). The elements of (APA) style: A survey of psychology journal editors. *American Psychologist, 56,* 266–267.

Cheung, C., & Ngai, S. S. (2007). Effective group work with delinquents in Hong Kong. *Adolescence, 42,* 151–165.

Children's Defense Fund (1994). *The state of America's children yearbook, 1994.* Washington, DC: Author.

Cohen, D., & Strayer, J. (1996). Empathy in conduct-disordered and comparison youth. *Developmental Psychology, 32,* 988–998.

Coleman, S. (2011). Addressing the puzzle of race. *Journal of Social Work Education, 47,* 91–108. doi:10.5175/JSWE.2011.200900086

College Board (2004). *Writing: A ticket to work ... or a ticket out* (2004). New York: Author. Retrieved January 2, 2007 from http://members.cox.net/graham. associates/writing-ticket-to-work.pdf

Cronin, K. L., Fazio, V. C., & Beins, B. C. (1998, April). Mood does not affect the funniness of jokes but jokes affect your mood. Presented at the Thirteenth Annual University of Scranton Psychology Conference, Scranton, PA.

Daniel, D. (2004, January). *How to use technology to ruin a perfectly good lecture.* Presentation at the annual National Institute on the Teaching of Psychology, St. Petersburg Beach, FL.

Deci, E. L., & Ryan, R. M. (1985). *Intrinsic motivation and self-determination in human behavior.* New York: Plenum.

Deci, E. L., & Ryan, R. M. (1991). A motivational approach to self: Integration in personality. In R. Dienstbier (Ed.), *Nebraska symposium on motivation:*

Vol. 38. *Perspectives on motivation* (pp. 237–288). Lincoln: University of Nebraska Press.

DePalma, M. T., Madey, S. F., Tillman, T. C., & Wheeler, J. (2000). Perceived patient responsibility and belief in a just world affect helping. *Basic and Applied Social Psychology, 21*, 131–137.

Dietz, A. P., Albowicz, C., & Beins, B. C. (2011, October). Neuroticism and sex-related jokes: Predictions from terror management theory. Poster session presented at the annual convention of the New England Psychological Association, Fairfield, CT.

Dutton, D. (1999, February 5). Language crimes: A lesson in how not to write,courtesy of the professoriate. *The Wall Street Journal.* Retrieved February 19, 2007 from http://denisdutton.com/language_crimes.htm

Enguidanos, S., Kogan, A. C., Keefe, B., Geron, S. M., & Katz, L. (2011). Patient-centered approach to building problem solving skills among older primary care patients: Problems identified and resolved. *Journal of Gerontological Social Work, 54*, 276–291. doi:10.1080/01634372.2011.552939

Eysenck, H. J. (1971). Personality and sexual adjustment. *British Journal of Psychiatry, 118*, 593–608.

Fairburn, C. B., Welch, S. L., Norman, P. A., O'Connor, B. A., & Doll, H. A. (1996). Bias and bulimia nervosa: How typical are clinical cases? *American Journal of Psychiatry, 153*, 386–391.

Felton, M., & Lyon, D. O. (1966). The post-reinforcement pause. *Journal of the Experimental Analysis of Behavior, 9*, 131–134.

Gallo, L. C., Troxel, W. M., Matthews, K. A., & Kuller, L. H. (2003). Marital status and quality in middle-aged women: Associations with levels and trajectories of cardiovascular risk factors. *Health Psychology, 22*(5), 453–463. doi:10.1037/0278-6133.22.5.453

Gerdes, K. E., Segal, E. A., Jackson, K. F., & Mullins, J. L. (2011). Teaching empathy: A framework rooted in social cognitive neuroscience and social justice. *Journal of Social Work Education, 47*, 109–131. doi:10.5175/JSWE.2011.200900085

Goldenberg, J. L., Pyszczynski, T. McCoy, K. M., Greenberg, J., & Solomon, S. (1999). Death, sex, love, and neuroticism: Why is sex such a problem? *Journal of Personality and Social Psychology, 77*, 1173–1187.

Grandey, A. A., Fisk, G. M., & Steiner, D. D. (2005). Must "Service With a Smile" Be Stressful? The Moderating Role of Personal Control for American and French Employees. *Journal of Applied Psychology, 90*, 893–904.

Gross, T., & Miller, D. (2006, May 17). Fresh Air [Radio broadcast]. Philadelphia, PA: National Public Radio.

Holland, A. (2007). Eureka! The importance of good science writing. Retrieved March 14, 2007 from http://www.writersblock.ca/winter2002/essay.htm

Huesmann, L. R., Moise-Titus, J., Podolski, C., & Eron, L. D. (2003). Longitudinal relations between children's exposure to TV violence and their aggressive and violent behavior in young adulthood: 1977–1992. *Developmental Psychology. Special Issue: Violent Children, 39*, 201–221. doi:10.1037/0012-1649.39.2.201

Huff, D. (1954). *How to lie with statistics.* New York: W. W. Norton.

Hyde, J. S. (2005). The gender similarities hypothesis. *American Psychologist, 60*, 581–592. doi:10.1037/0003-066X.60.6.581

Jackson, B., Kubzansky, L. D., & Wright, R. J. (2006). Linking perceived unfairness to physical health: The perceived unfairness model. *Review of General Psychology, 10*, 21–40. doi:10.1037/1089-2680.10.1.21

Jafari-Sabet, M. (2006). NMDA receptor blockers prevents the facilitatory effects of post-training intra-dorsal hippocampal NMDA and physostigmine on memory retention of passive avoidance learning in rats. *Behavioral Brain Research, 169*, 120–127.

Josselson, R., & Lieblich, A. (1996). Fettering the mind in the name of "science." *American Psychologist, 51*, 651–652.

Kaiser, C. R., Vick, S. B., & Major, B. (2006). Prejudice expectations moderate preconscious attention to cues that are threatening to social identity. *Psychological Science, 17*, 332–338.

Kanno, H., & Koeske, G. F. (2010). MSW students' satisfaction with their field placement: The role of preparedness and supervision quality. *Journal of Social Work Education, 46*, 23–38. doi:10.5175/JSWE.2010.200800066

Keegan, D. A., & Bannister, S. L. (2003). Effect of colour coordination of attire with poster presentation on poster popularity. *Canadian Medical Association Journal, 169*, 1291–1292.

Kendall, P. C., Silk, J. S., & Chu, B. C. (2000). Introducing your research report: Writing the introduction (pp. 41–57). In R. J. Sternberg, *Guide to publishing in psychology journals*, New York: Cambridge.

Klinesmith, J., Kasser, T., & McAndrew, F. T. (2006). Guns, testosterone, and aggression: An experimental test of a mediational hypothesis. *Psychological Science, 17*, 568–571.

Kolovelonis, A., Goudas, M., & Dermitzaki, I. (2011). The effect of different goals and self-recording on self-regulation of learning a motor skill in a physical education setting. *Learning and Instruction, 21*, 355–364. doi:10.1016/j.learninstruc.2010.04.001

Kruger, J., & Dunning, D. (1999). Unskilled and Unaware of It: How Difficulties in Recognizing One's Own Incompetence Lead to Inflated Self-Assessments. *Journal of Personality and Social Psychology, 77*, 121–134.

Ku, L., Dittmar, H., & Banerjee, R. (2011, September 26). Are Materialistic Teenagers Less Motivated to Learn? Cross-Sectional and Longitudinal Evidence From the United Kingdom and Hong Kong. *Journal of Educational Psychology.* Advance online publication. doi: 10.1037/a0025489

LaGreca, A. M., Silverman, W. K., Vernberg, E. M., & Prinstein, M. J. (1996). Symptoms of posttraumatic stress in children after Hurricane Andrew:

A prospective study. *Journal of Counseling and Clinical Psychology, 54,* 712–723.

Lann-Wolcott, H., Medvene, L. J., & Williams, K. (2011). Measuring the person-centeredness of caregivers working with nursing home residents with dementia. *Behavior Therapy, 42,* 89–99. doi:10.1016/j.beth.2010.02.005

Lightdale, J. R., & Prentice, D. A. (1994). Rethinking sex differences in aggression: Aggressive behavior in the absence of social roles. *Personality and Social Psychology Bulletin, 20,* 34–44. doi:10.1177/0146167294201003

Martin, J., & McGaffick, S. (2001, February). The effects of mood induction on humor appreciation. Poster presented at the University of Scranton Psychology Conference, Scranton, PA.

Matters, G., & Burnett, P. C. (2003). Psychological predictors of the propensity to omit short-response items on a high-stakes achievement test. *Educational and Psychological Measurement, 63,* 239–256.

McGrath, R. E. (2011). *Quantitative models in psychology.* Washington, DC: American Psychological Association.

Moscovice, L. R., & Snowdon, C. T. (2006). The role of social context and individual experience in novel task acquisition in cottontop tamarins, *Saguinus oedipus. Animal Behaviour, 71,* 933–943.

Petty, R. E. & Cacioppo, J. T. (1986). *Communication and persuasion: Central and peripheral routes to attitude change.* New York: Springer-Verlag.

Plous, S. (1996). Attitudes toward the use of animals in psychological research and education. *American Psychologist, 51,* 918–927.

Rader, N., & Vaughn, L. A. (2000). Infant reaching to a hidden affordance: Evidence for intentionality. *Infant Behavior & Development, 23,* 531–541.

Rank, O. (1932). *Art and artists: Creative urge and personality development.* New York: Knopf.

Rank, O. (1936). *Will therapy.* New York: Norton.

Reder, L. M., Oates, J. M., Thornton, E. R., Quinlan, J. J., Kaufer, A., & Sauer, J. (2006). Drug-induced amnesia hurts recognition, but only for memories that can be unitized. *Psychological Science, 17,* 562–567.

Rescorla, R. A. (2006). Deepened extinction from compound stimulus presentation. *Journal of Experimental Psychology: Animal Behavior Processes, 32,* 135–144.

Roediger, R. (2004, April). What should they be called? *APS Observer, 17.* Retrieved from http://www.psychologicalscience.org/observer/getArticle.cfm?id=1549

Rosenthal, R., & Fode, K. L. (1963). The effect of experimenter bias on the performance of the albino rat. *Behavioral Science, 8,* 183–189.

Rosnow, R. L., & Rosenthal, R. (1993). *Beginning behavioral research: A conceptual primer.* New York: Macmillan.

Russano, M. B., Meissner, C. A., Narchet, F. M., & Kassin, S. M. (2005). Investigating true and false confessions within a novel experimental paradigm. *Psychological Science, 16,* 481–486.

Salovey, P. (2000). Results that get results: Telling a good story. In R. J. Sternberg (Ed.), *Guide to publishing in psychology journals* (pp. 121–132). New York: Cambridge University Press.

Salsburg, D. (2002). *The lady tasting tea: How statistics revolutionized science in the twentieth century.* New York, NY: Holt Paperbacks.

Scheibe, C. L. (2004). A deeper sense of literacy: Curriculum-driven approaches to media literacy in the K-12 classroom. *The American Behavioral Scientist, 48,* 60–68.

Schmidt, K., & Diestel, S. (2011). Differential effects of decision latitude and control on the job demands–strain relationship: A cross-sectional survey study among elderly care nursing staff. *International Journal of Nursing Studies, 48,* 307–317. doi:10.1016/j.ijnurstu.2010.04.003

Schutte, N. S., Malouff, J. M., Hall, L. E., Haggerty, D. J., Cooper, J. T., Golden, C. J., & Dornheim, L. (1998). Development and validation of a measure of emotional intelligence. *Personality and Individual Differences, 25,* 167–177

Senecal, C., Vallerand, R. J., Guay, F. (2001). Antecedents and outcomes of work–family conflict: Toward a motivational model. *Personality and Social Psychology Bulletin, 27* 176–186.

Shatzman, K. B., & McQueen, J. M. (2006). Prosodic knowledge affects the recognition of newly acquired words. *Psychological Science, 17,* 372–377.

Sommer, R. (2006). Dual dissemination: Writing for colleagues and the public. *American Psychologist, 61,* 955–958.

Stephenson, H., Pena-Shaff, J., & Quirk, P. (2006). Predictors of college student suicidal ideation: Gender differences. *College Student Journal, 40,* 109–117.

Stephenson, J. H., Belesis, M. P., & Balliet, W. E. (2005). Variability in college student suicide: Age, gender, and race. *Journal of College Student Psychotherapy, 19,* 5–33. doi:10.1300/J035v19n04_02

Strick, M., Holland, R. W., van Baaren, R. B., & van Knippenberg, A. (2009). Finding comfort in a joke: Consolatory effects of humor through cognitive distraction. *Emotion, 9,* 574–578. doi:10.1037/a0015951

Swanson, H. L. (2011, August 22). Working Memory, Attention, and Mathematical Problem Solving: A Longitudinal Study of Elementary School Children. *Journal of Educational Psychology.* Advance online publication. doi: 10.1037/a0025114

Thomas, G. V., & Blackman, D. (1992). The future of animal studies in psychology. *American Psychologist, 47,* 1679.

Thompson, M. (2011). The best bang for our buck: Recommendations for the provision of training for tobacco action workers and indigenous health workers. *Contemporary Nurse, 37,* 90–91. doi:10.5172/conu.2011.37.1.090

Tufte, E. R. (1983). *The visual display of quantitative information.* Cheshire, CT: Graphics Press.

Uhlmann, E. L., & Cohen, G. L. (2005). Constructed criteria: Redefining merit to justify discrimination. *Psychological Science, 16*, 474–480.

Vorauer, J. D., & Sakamoto, Y. (2006). I thought we could be friends, but...: Systematic miscommunication and defensive distancing as obstacles to cross-group friendship formation. *Psychological Science, 17*, 326–331.

Wang, Q. (2006). Earliest recollections of self and others in European American and Taiwanese Young Adults. *Psychological Science, 17*, 708–714.

Wang, S., & Baillargeon, R. (2005). Inducing infants to detect a physical violation in a single trial. *Psychological Science, 16*, 542–549.

Warren, J. M. (1965). The comparative psychology of learning. *Annual Review of Psychology, 16*, 95–118.

Weary, G., Vaughn, L. A., Stewart, B. D., & Edwards, J. A. (2006). Adjusting for the correspondence bias: Effects of causal uncertainty, cognitive busyness, and causal strength of situational information. *Journal of Experimental Social Psychology, 42*, 87–94. doi:10.1016/j.jesp.2005.01.003

Wilkinson, L., & Task Force on Statistical Inference (1999). Statistical methods in psychology journals: Guidelines and explanations. *American Psychologist, 54*, 594–604.

Wimer, D. J., & Beins, B. C. (2000, August). Is this joke funny? Only if we say it is. Presented at the annual convention of the American Psychological Association. Washington, DC.

Wimer, D. J., & Beins, B. C. (2008). Expectation and perceived humor. *Humor: International Journal of Humor Studies, 21*(3), 347–363.

Winer, B. J., Brown, D. R., & Michels, K. M. (1991). *Statistical principles in experimental design* (3rd ed.). New York: McGraw Hill.

Zeidner, M., Shani-Zinovich, I., Matthews, G., & Roberts, R. D. (2005). Assessing emotional intelligence in gifted and non-gifted high school students: Outcomes depend on the measure. *Intelligence, 33*, 369–391.

Name Index

APA Style Simplified: Writing in Psychology, Education, Nursing, and Sociology,
First Edition. Bernard C. Beins.
© 2012 John Wiley & Sons, Inc. Published 2012 by John Wiley & Sons, Inc.

Subject Index

APA Style Simplified: Writing in Psychology, Education, Nursing, and Sociology,
First Edition. Bernard C. Beins.
© 2012 John Wiley & Sons, Inc. Published 2012 by John Wiley & Sons, Inc.